10/22

A SHORT GUIDE TO

PRAYING AS A FAMILY

GROWING TOGETHER
IN FAITH AND LOVE EACH DAY

D1122826

DOMINICAN SISTERS OF SAINT CECILIA CONGREGATION
NASHVILLE, TENNESSEE

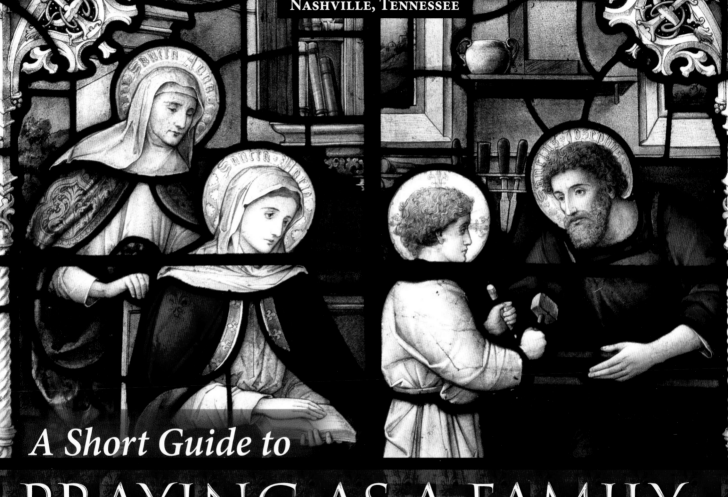

A Short Guide to

PRAYING AS A FAMILY

GROWING TOGETHER IN FAITH AND LOVE EACH DAY

Nihil Obstat: Thomas Joseph White, O.P., S.T.L., D. Phil.
Censor Librorum

Imprimatur: David R. Choby, D.D., J.C.L.
Bishop of Nashville
August 27, 2014

The Nihil Obstat and the Imprimatur are official declarations that a book or pamphlet is free of doctrinal and moral error. No implication is contained therein that those who have granted the Nihil Obstat and the Imprimatur agree with the opinions expressed.

Text © 2015 by St. Cecilia Congregation, LBP Communications. All rights reserved.
LBP Communications bases its name on the Dominican Order's motto, "*Laudare, Benedicere, Praedicare,*" which means "to praise, to bless, to preach."

All photographs of stained glass herein © 2015 by Father Lawrence Lew, O.P., unless otherwise noted. "The Stained Glass Tradition" © 2015 by Denis McNamara, Ph.D.

Scripture texts in this work are taken from the *New American Bible, revised edition* © 2010, 1991, 1986, 1970 Confraternity of Christian Doctrine, Washington, D.C. and are used by permission of the copyright owner. All rights reserved. No part of the New American Bible may be reproduced in any form without permission in writing from the copyright owner.
Excerpts from the English translation of the *Catechism of the Catholic Church* for use in the United States of America Copyright © 1994, United States Catholic Conference, Inc.—Libreria Editrice Vaticana. Used with Permission.

Every effort has been made to obtain and provide proper source attributions for selections in this volume. If any attribution is incorrect, the publisher welcomes written documentation supporting correction for subsequent printings.

No part of this book may be reproduced, stored in a retrieval system, or transmitted in any form, or by any means, electronic, mechanical, photocopying, or otherwise, without the prior written permission of the publisher.

Hardcover ISBN: 978-1-61890-682-3
Paperbound ISBN: 978-1-681890-683-0
eBook ISBN: 978-1-61890-684-7

Published in the United States by
Saint Benedict Press, LLC
PO Box 410487
Charlotte, NC 28241
www.SaintBenedictPress.com

Printed and bound in the United States of America

To Our Blessed Mother Mary,
Queen of Families,

Help of the Weak,
and Star of the New Evangelization

TABLE OF CONTENTS

LET HIM ENTER, THE KING OF GLORY!

FOREWORD

Archimedes, the ancient Greek scientist, once said that if he had a fulcrum and a long enough lever, one small man could move the world. Children and families are not levers. They're human beings. They're persons, not objects. But Archimedes' words are still useful. The formation that spouses give to each other and to their children—if it's done with love, courage, tenderness, and persistence—can move the world and change society.

This is why the greatest gift a father can give his children is to love their mother. And of course the same applies to mothers loving their husbands. Personal example is the most powerful teacher in the world. Children see everything, and they understand far more than adults often think. If parents love each other, children see and learn love. They learn *fidelity* instead of broken promises; *patience* instead of restlessness; *simplicity* in place of confusion; *humility* instead of pride; *courage* in place of cowardice; *honesty* instead of excuses; *forgiveness* in place of revenge; a *hunger for justice* in place of apathy.

And if parents love God, children see and learn faith. Parents who pray together teach by the way they live that God is real; that He is present, listening, and eager to be part of our lives. Helping children learn the habit of prayer thus becomes one of the most important lessons a family can share. A life of prayer makes us fully human because it makes us real; it brings us out of ourselves, again and again, into conversation with the Author of life Himself—the God who made and loves us, and created everything we know.

It's no secret that I've admired the Dominican Sisters of St. Cecilia for many years. The reason is simple. In the larger family of God we call the Church, the Sisters embody by their daily example every virtue that makes a family beautiful and filled with life. But they also teach by what they speak and write, edit and publish—and this volume, *A Short Guide to Praying as a Family*, is wonderful and very practical proof.

Archimedes never found the lever he needed. The Sisters remind us that Christian families already have one. Family prayer can move the world.

The Most Reverend Charles J. Chaput,
Archbishop of Philadelphia

TO THE GLORY OF GOD

ACKNOWLEDGMENTS

We would like to express our gratitude to Archbishop Charles J. Chaput, O.F.M. Cap., D.D., for his love and support of Catholic families and his support for this *Short Guide to Praying as a Family*. We would also like to thank our own Bishop, David R. Choby, D.D., J.C.L., for his outstanding leadership and guidance. Our special thanks go to Father Lawrence Lew, O.P., Denis R. McNamara, Ph.D., Father Thomas Joseph White, O.P., D.Phil., Melvin Laurel, J.D., Lisa Julia Hill-Sutton, Virginia Raguin, Ph.D., the Richard and Margaret Kennedy Family, Richard and Maureen Herman, the Paul E. Husak Family, and Aquinas College (Nashville), who have helped to make this book possible. We are grateful for all the families we serve as well as those we have had the privilege of serving. Finally, we are most grateful to our own parents, who first taught us how to pray.

She saith unto him Rabboni which is to say Master

INTRODUCTION:
HOW TO USE THIS BOOK

Prayer is as simple and natural as friendship. It is loving conversation with the Lord, with Him whom we know loves us.[1] It is raising our hearts and our minds to Him. Prayer *is* our relationship with the living and present God.[2]

Beginning to pray as a family can genuinely transform your life, enriching not only your relationship with the Lord but also your relationships with one another. Prayer can change the way you see the ordinary circumstances of your daily life. You begin to see disappointments as perhaps God's way of leading you to new and better opportunities, joys as a share in the life of heaven, and sufferings as a way to enter into the mystery of Jesus' own suffering for us on the Cross. The closer we are to the Lord in prayer, the more we realize that He is present with us, walks with us, in our daily lives. We begin to see as He sees and to love as He loves. Thank you for your faith. Thank you for picking up this book, for desiring to draw your whole family closer to God. "[T]he Lord takes pleasure in those . . . who put their hope in his mercy" (cf. Ps 147:11), and "[t]he

Lord is good . . . to the one that seeks him" (cf. Lam 3:25).

Through prayer we nourish our personal relationship with God, much as fertilizer and weeding, water and sunshine, nourish a garden. Thus, it is not surprising that Christian writers have often compared the soul to a garden. Beautiful gardens are a delight. The brilliance of the palette of colors, the sweet scents, the restful shade, the tranquil silence, all make a garden the perfect place to rest, to be still. Your hearts (the hearts of the members of your family) are that garden in which you can rest with the Lord and He can rest with you. However, gardens require a great deal of constant care: planning, tilling, planting, weeding, watering, pruning, and fertilizing. That's where this book comes in. The types of prayer in this book contain each of these components. Some are like flowering or fruit-bearing plants; others are like bushes or groundcover; still others are the water, the pruning, or the fertilizing. For instance, Going to Confession as a Family (page 103) is the equivalent of weeding your garden. You don't want weeds to take over, so you won't want to neglect that crucial component of family prayer! Confession also brings

---

[1] cf. St. Teresa of Avila, *The Way of Perfection.*
[2] cf. *Catechism of the Catholic Church,* 2558.

marvelous new graces and gifts to your family. God is the Master Gardener; we simply need to cooperate with His grace, and allow Him to prune and water the garden of our souls. He will give us new growth.

As you'll notice from the Table of Contents, this book is organized according to phases. Phase One contains the Basic Vocal Prayers: the Sign of the Cross, the Our Father, the Hail Mary, and the Glory Be. These are the staples, the plants you want to have all over your garden. Phase Two guides you in Making Your Home a Sacred Place, unifying your family in the desire to have the Lord as the center and goal of your family.

The remaining phases allow you to continue your growth in prayer. Take a moment to look at the progression of the phases in the Table of Contents. Remember, as you do so, that your family does not need to do everything that is listed. You can customize the phases according to your family's needs and preferences. If you do begin to try one type of prayer (for instance, Preparing for Mass as a Family), try it several times before deciding whether or not that prayer is a "fit" for your family. Prayer takes practice, so give yourselves a chance to become comfortable with a particular form of prayer before you give up on it.

Please remember that merely *saying* the prayers is not the goal. The goal is *praying*: personally encountering the Lord, listening to Him, and giving Him your heart. Formal prayers and methods of prayer are intended as a *means* to help us in our own personal conversation with the Lord: to come to know Him and to speak to Him in our own words, as one speaks with a friend. By praying, we learn how to listen to Him—how to be docile to His promptings and attentive to His way of seeing reality. He is always with us. Through prayer we learn more and more how to be with Him. The words of the prayers help to form our hearts and minds, so when we pray them as a family, they express our shared life with one another and with the Lord—a unity and a desire for greater unity with and in Him.

Many of the prayers in this book are handed down to us through tradition; Christians have been praying them for hundreds of years. Just as these formal prayers have helped them to begin praying, showing them how to speak to the Lord, they do the same for us, drawing us into a deeper and deeper relationship with the Lord. Thus, when we come together for communal prayer (such as the Holy Sacrifice of the Mass), the prayers in our tradition give us the words to pray as a community and as a Church. If we have a deep relationship with the Lord, these prayers are more than mere words—they become communal conversations with the Lord, who is the center of our community, our families, and our Church. Ultimately, what is important is that we talk with the Lord, listen to Him, and allow Him to speak to us through the Scriptures and to pour out His graces upon us through the sacraments.

Each prayer in this book is followed by pages that explain the prayer (how it forms our minds and hearts) and suggest appropriate times or other ideas for that particular prayer. You can use the explanations to help your children understand the meaning and purpose of each prayer. Each phase builds on the phases that go before it. Hopefully, your family will look forward to entering each new phase as your prayer life develops and you grow closer to the Lord.

May the garden of your family's hearts remain always in bloom, inviting and pleasing to Our Lord. May your family be the garden where Christ Himself is always welcome, where He always delights, and where He always rests. May He, the Master-Gardener, be the One who applies His gentle artistry to water (to bless), to prune (to purify), and to give new growth to your whole family. He longs for you. He longs to be welcome in your family, to rest in the garden of your souls, a place of peace and beauty within. As this begins to happen in your own family, may you bring the precious gift of praying as a family to other families.

A FEW PRACTICAL NOTES

Family life is so busy these days, and many demands are made on our time, yet this is precisely what makes praying together so important. When God is at the center of our family life, all our other priorities fall into place. We put God first, and our spouse and children next. Extended family and work follow after these. Children learn to put their brothers and sisters before their friends, and to put attending Mass before other activities. When your family prays together, you are not only putting God at the center of your family, but also showing your children how to enter into a personal relationship with Him so that He becomes a companion and friend throughout life.

The most effective way to begin implementing family prayer is to build it into your schedule, that is, to pray in the course of things you already do. For example, you already get in the car to go somewhere, so you can easily add saying the Angel of God prayer (page 81) shortly after you get in the car. You also already eat meals together, so you can easily add praying Grace Before and After Meals (page 47). Filling your day with prayer fills your day with awareness of the Lord's presence, goodness, and love.

In the course of implementing the prayers you choose, we encourage you to be careful and gentle, because you don't want your children or your spouse to develop a distaste for prayer. You want family prayer to be a positive experience. Also remember that everything doesn't have to be perfect. Little ones are going to squirm. Teens may act as if they don't care. Others may be experiencing withdrawal from hyper-connectivity (to the television, computer games, electronic devices, cell phones, etc.). Be at peace yourself and keep peace in the family. Don't be discouraged. Be forgiving of yourself and your family if you get off track. Life can also seem to take you off track. So, when there is a change in the routine, simply adjust your prayer. Ask the Lord how to do it. For instance, if you are traveling in the car, and it is time for Family Bedtime Prayers, you may want to pray them in the car and shorten them for the sake of the exhausted members of your family. A simple movement of the heart toward the Lord in gratitude and love is a thousand times better than many words spoken only from a sense of duty.

Try your best to pray together, "[f]or where two or three are gathered together in my name, there am I in the midst of them" (Mt 18:20). Discuss the prayers you are choosing to pray together. Get your children involved, especially the older ones, asking their advice and their ideas. Everyone likes to be included. If you believe you may experience resistance from your teens, speak to them privately first and ask them what they think about beginning to pray together as a family. Listen to them. You might even want to ask them to lead some of the prayers. Or, in other cases, you may want to give them the option to come or not to come, but let them know you would like for them to come since they are important members of the family. When your family makes the time and the effort to pray, you will be blessed by the Lord. He meets our weakness with His mercy and love. He will reward your generosity with His infinite generosity.

Finally, remember the power of community. You are not alone. There are over one billion Catholics in the world! There is another family in your neighborhood or in your parish that would also like to start praying together. Why not find two or more friends who have this same desire, and support one another in working together to implement praying with your families? You might even start a small parish group for this purpose. You can be a source of encouragement for one another, and you can share your experiences and concerns, receiving advice and reassurance from one another.

We hope these pages will help your family to grow in love for God and one another, for your faith and for your life of prayer. We hope they will help you to teach your children about the beauty and meaning of life, about how to love and be loved, by God and by each other. As you journey along and deepen your relationship with the Lord, may the treasured Catholic prayers in this book accompany you, so that your family—a domestic church—will always be united to God in love.

PHASE ONE

BASIC VOCAL PRAYERS

The Sign of the Cross

The Our Father

The Hail Mary

The Glory Be

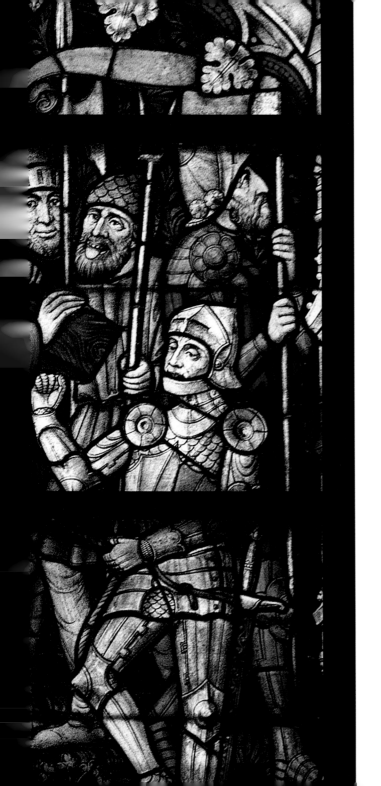

THE SIGN OF
THE CROSS

In the name of the Father,
and of the Son,
and of the Holy Spirit.
Amen.

Making the Sign of the Cross is a prayer. The Cross is the symbol of Christianity, for it is on the Cross that Christ shows His love for us by dying for us, saving us from sin and death. Moreover, through the Sign of the Cross, we invoke the Three Persons of the Holy Trinity: the Father, the Son, and the Holy Spirit. Thus, two of the greatest mysteries of our faith—the Holy Trinity and our redemption by Christ on the Cross—are encompassed by this one prayer. Even as early as the 5th Century, Christians began making a large Sign of the Cross over themselves[1] in a way very similar to the way we Christians do today. Because of its intense store of meaning, the Sign of the Cross has traditionally been used to begin and end every prayer, including the greatest prayer, the Holy Mass.

Traditionally, the Sign of the Cross is made in this manner: at the words, "In the name of the Father," the Christian touches the fingers of the right hand to the forehead; at the words, "and of the Son," the hand is moved downwards (drawing, in effect, the vertical crossbeam); at the words, "and of the Holy" the fingers touch the left shoulder; at the word, "Spirit," the right shoulder (drawing the horizontal crossbeam).

Finally, the hands are joined together with the word "Amen" (which means, "truly it is so" or "so be it").

Children can easily be taught to understand the meaning of these gestures as saying to God: "Take my mind" (when we put our fingers to our foreheads); "Take my heart" (when we move our fingers over our hearts); and, "Take my whole self" (when we touch our fingers to each shoulder).

Teach your children to make the Sign of the Cross with reverence, attention, and love, for this prayer is a beautiful proclamation of our faith in Jesus Christ and all He has done for us. Sometimes we feel rushed or do not want to hold others up by taking the time to wait for our children, particularly small children, to make the Sign of the Cross, and we can assume that eventually they'll catch on. However, waiting and modeling the Sign of the Cross, even with toddlers, is worth all the time in the world. Allowing the smallest children to participate in our family prayers by sharing in this gesture of faith is a powerful way to include them in the family prayer. It is perhaps easiest to show young children how to make the Sign of the Cross by standing or kneeling behind them and moving the child's hand slowly through the steps of the Sign of

---

[1] *New Catholic Encyclopedia,* 2nd ed., s.v. "Sign of the Cross."

the Cross as you recite the words aloud. Or, one parent can demonstrate in mirror-image fashion (that is using the opposite hand and doing the opposite gesture that the child mirrors in making the Sign of the Cross) in front of the child while the other parent helps the child from behind. Older children can also help the younger ones to make the Sign of the Cross.

A valuable practice is making the Sign of the Cross right after you wake up in the morning. With this simple prayer, you give your entire day to the Lord and ask Him to be your shield, your protector. Children very easily understand this concept: the Sign of the Cross is like putting on your holy armor for the day.

23

THE OUR FATHER

Our Father, who art in heaven,
hallowed be Thy name.
Thy kingdom come.
Thy will be done,
on earth as it is in heaven.
Give us this day our daily bread,
and forgive us our trespasses,
as we forgive those
who trespass against us.
And lead us not into temptation,
but deliver us from evil.
Amen.

Jesus Himself taught us the "Our Father" ("the Lord's Prayer") while He was on earth (cf. Mt 6:9-13). In it He shows us how to address God. He does not tell us to call Him "Master," or "Your Highness," for neither of these names captures adequately the relationship God has with us. God desires for us to be His children. We accept this tremendous gift by calling Him "Father." United to Jesus, we pray, "Our Father." As a family we pray, "Our Father."

Seven fundamental petitions make up the Our Father. We ask that God's name be hallowed or reverenced; that His kingdom be in our midst (by His presence and by the way we live united to Him); that we do what He asks of us (as the angels and saints do in heaven); that He give us the food we need (both ordinary food and the extraordinary food of the Eucharist); that He forgive us our sins just as we strive truly to forgive those who hurt or offend us; that He preserve us from being tempted to sin; and that He save us from sin, evil, and the works of the devil.

Because Our Lord Jesus Christ gave this prayer to us Himself, it is traditionally considered the most powerful prayer against evil as well as the most perfect prayer.

When you pray this prayer, first begin with the Sign of the Cross. Then, pray the Our Father. Finally, close with the Sign of the Cross. You can pray this prayer together as a family before going to sleep at night. This prayer can also be used at any time throughout the day when you need to pray for some particular intention.

AND THE WORD
BECAME FLESH
AND MADE HIS DWELLING
AMONG US,
AND WE SAW HIS GLORY,
THE GLORY AS OF THE
FATHER'S ONLY SON,
FULL OF GRACE AND TRUTH.

JOHN 1:14

THE HAIL MARY

Hail Mary, full of grace,
the Lord is with thee.
Blessed art thou among women,
and blessed is the fruit of thy womb, Jesus.
Holy Mary, Mother of God,
pray for us sinners now
and at the hour of our death.
Amen.

While she was carrying Jesus in her womb, Mary went to visit her cousin, Elizabeth, who was also pregnant at the time. When Elizabeth heard Mary's voice from a distance, the child in Elizabeth's womb leapt for joy, leading Elizabeth to understand the mysterious and glorious presence of God in Mary's womb. Mary was especially chosen by God to be the Mother of Jesus. Thus, Elizabeth greeted Mary with the words: "[B]lessed are you among women, and blessed is the fruit of your womb" (Lk 1:42).

Mary is a simple human being just like us, but what makes her so worthy of our praise and imitation is her "Yes" to what the Lord was asking of her. Just as she did, we daily receive the grace to say "Yes" to God and all that He asks. But, do we accept that grace as completely as she did? The more we say "Yes" to God, the more holy we become. It is not easy always to say "Yes" to what God is asking of us, to the people and the circumstances of our lives, but Mary never failed to do this. Mary never sinned. Moreover, because she is Jesus' mother and because Jesus is God, Mary is also called "the Mother of God."

No human being is closer to Jesus Christ than His mother, Mary. And, since the Scriptures tell us to "pray for one another" (Jas 5:16) and to ask others to pray for us, we ask those

Hail, Mary, full of grace. These five words announce the dawn of our salvation. They are the first words spoken by the Angel Gabriel to the young Jewish girl, Mary, as he asked her whether or not she would be willing to become the Mother of Jesus Christ, the Son of God (cf. Lk 1:26-38). Mary said "Yes" to God, "Yes" to carrying, giving birth to, and nurturing Jesus Christ as her Son. The Lord prepared her for this role by filling her with grace. She is the Immaculate Conception, born without original sin and full of grace.

who are close to God to pray for us. How much more ought we to ask the Mother of Jesus to pray for us? We ask her to ask Jesus to give us the graces and blessings we need. When we have any need, we can ask for Mary's help in praying for us. We will most especially need her help "at the hour of our death," in the moment when we are dying. Temptations can be especially strong at that time, and so we ask for Mary's most powerful help and protection in that last hour of our lives and the lives of all the members of our family. We are also asking Mary to be there to comfort us, just as she comforted Jesus by being there for Him in His last hours as He was dying on the Cross.

When you pray this prayer, first begin with the Sign of the Cross. Then, pray the Hail Mary. Finally, close with the Sign of the Cross. If you are saying the Our Father as a family before going to sleep at night, you can also pray the Hail Mary immediately afterwards. When you pray more than one prayer in a row, it is customary to open the series of prayers with the Sign of the Cross, pray the prayers (two or more), and then close with the Sign of the Cross. The Hail Mary can also be prayed at any time throughout the day. For instance, some families will pray it when they are driving and hear an ambulance or see an accident, asking Mary to help all those involved, especially those in danger of death. You can pray the Hail Mary for anyone, anything, or any event that you believe could use Mary's help.

THE GLORY BE

Glory be to the Father,
and to the Son, and to the Holy Spirit,
as it was in the beginning
is now and ever shall be,
world without end.
Amen.

This ancient prayer of praise is related to the song of the angels at the birth of Christ, "Glory to God in the highest" (Lk 2:14). Both offer exultant praise and thanksgiving to the entire Trinity: Father, Son, and Holy Spirit. Of all creatures, only humans and angels can speak and sing praise to God. The sun, the moon, the trees, the seas, the mountains, and the beaches have no voice; so we lend them our voices by lifting them up in praise to God (cf. Dan 3:57-88).

This simple and beautiful prayer, like the Sign of the Cross, draws our attention to the central mystery of our faith—the Most Holy Trinity. We believe in One God (One Divine Nature) in Three Divine Persons. Our Triune God wanted the human family to be an image of the love-giving and life-giving communion of Persons within the Most Holy Trinity. It is this communion of Persons that we praise when we pray the beautiful Glory Be. After you pray the Glory Be or any other prayer, always feel free to speak to God in your own words about anything on your mind or heart.

When you pray the Glory Be, begin and end with the Sign of the Cross. If, as a family, you are praying the Our Father and the Hail Mary before going to sleep at night, the Glory Be would be the perfect prayer to complete your set of bedtime prayers. When you pray more than one prayer in a row, it is customary to open the series of prayers with the Sign of the Cross, pray the prayers (in this case, the Our Father, the Hail Mary, and the Glory Be), and then close with the Sign of the Cross.

The Glory Be can also be prayed at any time throughout the day. For instance, it is a practice to pray the Glory Be as a prayer of thanksgiving to God for something good (big or small) that has happened: a child's birth, a small success, a lovely day, a safe trip, etc. To pray the Glory Be in thanksgiving, you may pray a single Glory Be or choose to pray it three times. This series of three is traditionally understood as honoring each of the Three Persons in the Trinity. By praying the Glory Be, you and your family grow in recognizing that every good thing comes from the Lord.

THE BEST IDEAL IS THE TRUE
AND OTHER TRUTH IS NONE.
ALL GLORY BE ASCRIBED TO
THE HOLY THREE IN ONE.

Gerard Manley Hopkins

This stained glass window depicts a typical symbol presenting the Mystery of the Trinity: the word "God" (Deus) is in the center. The word "Father" (Pater) is above to the left. Linking the words "Father" and "God" is the word "is" (est). The Father is God. The same is repeated for the word "Son"(Filius) to the right and the word "Holy Spirit" (Sanctus Spiritus) at the bottom, for the Son is God and the Holy Spirit is God. Finally, between the Persons, are the words "is not" (non est) for the Father is not the Son; the Son is not the Holy Spirit; and the Holy Spirit is not the Father. The Three Persons have the same Divine Nature, but They are distinct from One Another.

PHASE TWO

MAKING YOUR HOME A SACRED PLACE

CREATING SACRED SPACES IN YOUR HOME

MORNING OFFERING

GRACE AT MEALS

FAMILY BEDTIME PRAYERS

MONTHLY FAMILY MEETING

PRAYING WITH YOUR SPOUSE

THE FAMILY ROSARY

CREATING SACRED SPACES IN YOUR HOME

PRAYER OF CONSECRATION TO THE SACRED HEART OF JESUS AND THE IMMACULATE HEART OF MARY

Most Sacred Heart of Jesus and Immaculate Heart of Mary,
we consecrate our whole family to You.
We consecrate all that You have given us:
our lives, each member of our family,
our gifts and talents, our sorrows and joys,
our home and all our possessions.
We beg You to use us to show forth Your love and Your glory.
Help us in our weakness and selfishness,
so that we may persevere, faithful to You, to the end of our lives.

May we love You more and more each day
and long to encounter You, Jesus, in the sacraments.
May we serve You by serving one another, neighbor, and country.
Accept, O Most Sacred Heart of Jesus
and Immaculate Heart of Mary,
our humble offering of our family to You.
Be with us always—in every trial, difficulty, and suffering.
In You we hope.
Amen.[1]

Most Sacred Heart of Jesus, have mercy on us.
Immaculate Heart of Mary, pray for us.

---

[1] Composed by the Dominican Sisters of St. Cecilia. With the ecclesiastical approval of the Most Reverend David R. Choby, D.D., J.C.L., Bishop of Nashville, on December 9, 2014.

As you begin to pray more and more as a family, your home itself becomes a place of prayer, a sacred space. Perhaps there is one area of your home in particular where you pray together, or perhaps there is a place you would like set aside as a place of prayer where any family member can go to pray. An ideal place is oftentimes around the fireplace, in a corner of the living room or family room, or any comfortable place in your home where your family likes to gather. There, you could mount a large crucifix and place statues of the Blessed Virgin Mary, Saint Joseph, and other saints who may be special to your family. For example, if you have a child named Sebastian, you could have a statue of St. Sebastian. This sacred space could also have the family Bible, rosaries, and other holy images and sacred items (such as relics and holy water). The family prayer board (see page 120) could later be added in or placed close to this area. Candles can further beautify the sacred space, reminding your family of the light and warmth brought by God's presence in your home. The children can also place flowers in this space. You might have them take turns making sure there are always fresh flowers.

In making a sacred place in your home, allow every family member to give input. Let it be a family project. You may be amazed at the ideas your children come up with. It may

be important to also set rules about the sacred space (e.g., no electronics).

You may want to create smaller sacred spaces in each child's bedroom. This, too, would be an appropriate place for a crucifix (e.g., above your child's bed) and for the child's saint to be represented somehow. You might also place the child's baptismal candle and rosary there. A simple but beautiful image of the Blessed Virgin Mary and the child's Bible might also be placed there; or allow your children to create their own sacred spaces in their rooms.

These sacred spaces in our homes invite us to turn our minds and hearts to God more often and to recognize His presence in our daily lives. They encourage us to call upon Him and His saints, as well as to thank Him for the many blessings we receive from His hands each day.

Many families also choose to consecrate ("set apart" or "dedicate") their homes and their families to the Sacred Heart of Jesus and the Immaculate Heart of Mary. This means that they choose for their families to belong in a special way to Jesus and Mary, to receive their powerful protection and help. Through the consecration, the family also promises to try to live for God's glory and honor. The devotion to the Sacred (or "Holy") Heart of

Jesus was spread through the work and prayer of St. Margaret Mary Alacoque (1647-1690). By thinking about the Heart of Jesus, we can come to a better understanding of His true humanity and His love for us. Jesus Christ, the Son of God, has a real human heart. With His Sacred Heart, He loves us. It was this Sacred Heart that was pierced by a lance while Jesus hung on the Cross (cf. Jn 19:34). Devotion to the Immaculate Heart of Mary became widespread shortly after Pope Pius XII consecrated the whole world to Mary's Immaculate Heart in 1942.[2] Mary has a human heart, and hers is the heart most closely united to Jesus' Heart. Her heart is "immaculate," or "without stain," because Mary has never sinned and was conceived without original sin. Purity, goodness, mercy, gentleness, and love are all characteristics of Mary's heart. Mary loves us, her children, with her Immaculate Heart.

If you would like to consecrate your home and family to the Sacred Heart of Jesus and the Immaculate Heart of Mary, you may do so using the prayer given on page 38. This prayer may be prayed by your entire family or by you and your spouse. You may pray it just once, or once a year, once a month, or as often as you would like. Once your home is consecrated, you may display an image of the Sacred Heart of Jesus and of the Immaculate Heart of Mary. This is a lovely way to honor Jesus and Mary.

I AM GOING TO PREPARE
A PLACE FOR YOU.

JOHN 14:2

---

[2] *New Catholic Encyclopedia,* s.v. "Immaculate Heart of Mary."

MORNING OFFERING

O Jesus, through the
Immaculate Heart of Mary,
I offer you all my prayers, works, joys,
and sufferings of this day,
for all the intentions of your Sacred Heart,
in union with the Holy Sacrifice of the Mass
throughout the world,
in reparation for my sins,
for the conversion of sinners,
and for the intentions of Our Holy Father
this month.
Amen.[1]

---

[1] This prayer, composed by Father Francois Xavier Gaulrelet in 1844, is a familiar form of the Morning Offering currently in use in the United States (cf. *Encyclopedia of Catholic Devotions and Practices*, s.v. "Morning Offering").

From the earliest days of Christianity, the followers of Christ understood that they were to unite the sacrifice of their lives to Christ's sacrifice of His life on the Cross. Christ died once for all on the Cross, and we Christians are called to "die" to self daily—rejecting sin and selfishness; accepting difficulties, hardships, and inconveniences with patience; giving to others with kindness and generosity, even against our own personal preferences; and, bearing with Christ the personal injuries inflicted upon us by the insensitivity or cruelty of others.

However, our days on earth also participate in the beauty and glory of Christ's Resurrection. We have the joys and blessings of daily life, of marriage, of family, of people who love and care about us. We have food, shelter, clothing, comforts, and the wonderful gift of faith. We have all the gifts offered to us by the Catholic Church—the sacraments, our friends, our parishes, and all the goods of parish life. Recognizing that all things come to us from God and desiring to thank Him for them, we offer ourselves to God by offering Him each day and everything in it through the Morning Offering.

By beginning your family's day with the Morning Offering, you make your whole day holy, united to Jesus and Mary and to the Holy Sacrifice of the Mass. Your whole day becomes a prayer for others, for the forgiveness of your sins, for the conversion of sinners, and for the intentions of the Pope, who knows the needs of the Church throughout the world.

Before going off to school or work, offer your day to the Lord together as a family. You can pray this prayer as a family right before breakfast, or right after breakfast and before everyone heads out the door. This way, you will remain united to each other and the Lord throughout the day.

FOR WHERE
TWO OR THREE
ARE GATHERED
TOGETHER
IN MY NAME,
THERE
AM I
IN THE MIDST
OF THEM.

MATTHEW 18:20

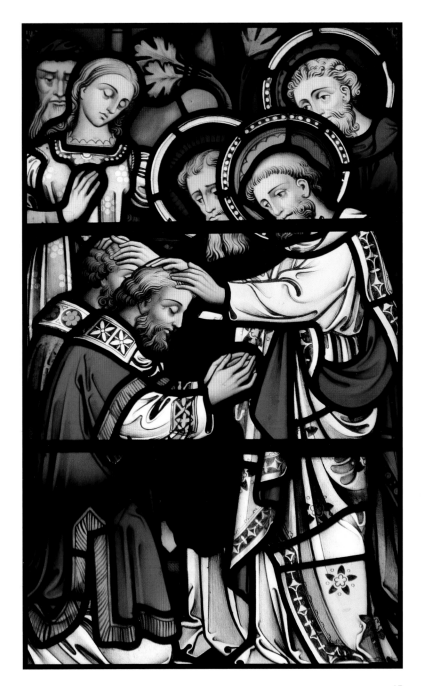

GRACE AT MEALS

GRACE BEFORE MEALS

Bless us, O Lord, and these Thy gifts,
which we are about to receive,
from Thy bounty,
through Christ, Our Lord.
Amen.

GRACE AFTER MEALS

We give Thee thanks, Almighty God,
for these and all Thy benefits,
who lives and reigns forever and ever.
May the souls of the faithful departed,
through the mercy of God,
rest in peace.
Amen.

SO WHETHER
YOU EAT OR DRINK,
OR WHATEVER YOU DO,
DO EVERYTHING
FOR THE
GLORY OF GOD.

1 CORINTHIANS 10:31

According to an ancient legend, a mother pelican saved her dying young by piercing her own breast and feeding them with her blood. She died to give them life. Christians adopted the pelican as a symbol of Christ, for He gives us His Blood in the Eucharist, and He dies to give us life.

Since the time of the Apostles, Christians have prayed prayers of "grace" (that is, "thanks") before and after meals, recognizing that God is the Giver and the Sustainer of life.

A family meal is a sacred event. Eating together as a family gives us a sense of the joy of belonging to one another and to God, the Giver of all good things. Thus, coming together at a meal is the perfect time to thank Him not only for our food but also for each other. In the Sacred Scriptures, we find that sharing a meal is a sign of communion, of unity. By sitting down to eat, we acknowledge our need for food to sustain our life. Eating and drinking are our most basic needs. But when, as a loving family, we sit down to eat together, we also take part in conversation, sharing our joys, our hopes, our worries, and our struggles. So, while we are eating and drinking, we often share our highest aspirations as well as the ordinariness of our day. It is for these reasons that family meals are so important and so enriching. They truly symbolize and are a sharing of life—of the food that gives life, and of the love and caring about one another that give meaning to life. This food for our bodies and this food for our souls are what Christ wants us to share. He is the Guest always present and welcome at our tables. He is the One who gives us food, shelter, and the blessings of life and family. Praying Grace before and after meals, even in public, expresses our awareness of Him and our gratitude.

Once everyone is seated at the table and ready, make the Sign of the Cross. Pray together the Grace Before Meals. Close with the Sign of the Cross. After the meal is finished but before everyone stands, make the Sign of the Cross. Pray together the Grace After Meals, and then close with the Sign of the Cross.

You will notice that in the Grace After Meals there is a special prayer for the deceased. This Catholic custom enables us to remember each day to pray for those who have died, especially our relatives and friends. In fact, the Scriptures also contain examples of St. Paul and other faithful men praying for the souls of the dead (cf. 2 Tm 1:16-18 and 2 Mc 12:39-45). The Grace Before and After Meals is also a time when you can extemporaneously add short little prayers asking God for whatever your family or the world may need. Commonly added are prayers such as the following: "God bless the cook!"; "May the Lord bless those who go without food today;" "Please bless [a person is named];" etc. It is also appropriate to add special prayers of thanks, such as, "Thank you, Lord, for Grandma's successful surgery;" or, "Thank you, Lord, for a good first day of school;" etc.

The Grace Before and After Meals is also a concrete way to practice and hand on the truth that our faith and our family values are not just for when we are home but are a part of all of our life. We do not need to be showy nor should we be, but simply making the Sign of the Cross and praying Grace Before and after Meals when we are together as a family at home, or even in a restaurant or at a picnic, is not only consistent with our faith that God is a part of every aspect of our life, but it is also a simple yet powerful witness of our Christian faith that we can give to others.

I AM
THE LIVING BREAD
THAT CAME DOWN
FROM HEAVEN. . . .
UNLIKE YOUR
ANCESTORS WHO ATE
AND STILL DIED,
WHOEVER EATS
THIS BREAD
WILL LIVE FOREVER.

JOHN 6:51, 58

FAMILY
BEDTIME PRAYERS

O God, you are my God—
it is you I seek! . . .
I look to you in the sanctuary
to see your power and glory.

For your love is better than life;
my lips shall ever praise you!
I will bless you as long as I live;
I will lift up my hands,
calling on your name. . . .

I think of you upon my bed,
I remember you through the watches
of the night.

You indeed are my savior,
and in the shadow of your wings
I shout for joy.
My soul clings fast to you;
your right hand upholds me.

PSALM 63:2-5, 6-9

A nightly ritual of praying together as a family before you tuck your children into bed can be one of the happy and precious memories you give to your children. Imagine how well they will sleep, secure in your love and secure in God's love.

Once all have brushed their teeth, put on their pajamas, etc., and are ready for bed, you can follow this simple format for bedtime prayers:

1. The family gathers in a comfortable place.

2. When everyone is settled, Dad begins with the Sign of the Cross.

3. Then, each family member (either in age order or beginning with Mom or Dad) does the following:

    a. Gives thanks for one specific thing (e.g., "Thank you, God, for our cousins' visit today.")

    b. Mentions one special intention that all can pray for (e.g., "Jesus, please help Granddad to get better." Or, "For Uncle Mike's surgery.")

4. Next, all together say one Hail Mary for their vocation (a vocation is that special calling from God for your life in the future;

each child will have a unique vocation—it could be to marriage, priesthood, religious life, or to the dedicated single life). Close together with the Sign of the Cross.

5. Finally, each member of the family goes to every other member of the family (in no particular order and with some degree of happy chaos) and

    a. Traces a Cross on the other person's forehead (as a sign calling down God's blessing on that person)

    b. Gives the other person a hug or kiss good night.

This is a wonderful way to end your day. Moreover, it also helps you as parents to know the things that are important to each of your children. For instance, you see that your oldest son loves his cousins because that is what came out in his thanksgiving prayer; you see the things that they worry about, through the fact that your youngest daughter prayed for Uncle Mike during the intentions. If you choose to follow the above format for your Family Bedtime Prayers, you can replace the Our Father, Hail Mary, and Glory Be you were saying with the prayers above, or you can continue to pray them together in addition to the above.

SLEEPLESS NIGHTS, QUIET TIMES, AND EXAMENS

Sleepless nights or other quiet times are perfect for helping to form your children's hearts and minds. During these quiet times, parents can do a sort of examination of the day, helping their children to see the blessings of the day, God's grace, difficult times, or mistakes, and to place it all back in the hands of God. The conversation is as easy as asking, "So, how was your day today?" "What did you do today?" If perhaps they played with an older brother or sister or did something special, you can ask, "Why do you think Johnny did that for you?" Lead them to recognize that action as a gift and an act of love. Then lead them to thank God for that act of goodness, and ask a blessing on the person who was good to them.

Perhaps they played outside or with a new toy. Lead them to see the blessing of their health, the beautiful day, or the generosity of others. Lead them to thank God for these blessings or to pray for those who do not have as much as they do. If they had something difficult happen (such as getting into a fight with a sibling over a toy or hurting someone's feelings), this is the perfect opportunity to teach them how to "walk in someone else's shoes." Let them share their feelings, and then ask them how they think the other person felt. Help them to identify what was "broken" in the relationship: feelings, trust, etc., and talk about ways to mend what is broken. Talk about options for handling similar situations in the future.

Lead them to pray for the other person and for their relationship.

End by thanking God for the blessings of the day and asking for the grace to stay near Him and to love Him tomorrow.

MONTHLY FAMILY MEETING

The Lord is my shepherd;
there is nothing I lack.
In green pastures he makes me lie down;
to still waters he leads me;
he restores my soul.
He guides me along right paths
for the sake of his name.
Even though I walk through
the valley of the shadow of death,
I will fear no evil, for you are with me;
your rod and your staff comfort me.

You set a table before me
in front of my enemies;
You anoint my head with oil;
my cup overflows.
Indeed, goodness and mercy will pursue me
all the days of my life;
I will dwell in the house of the Lord
for endless days.

Psalm 23

The members of your family are the most important people in your life. Make time for them. Help them to make time for each other. Families that are close are close because of the time they spend together, the things they share together, and the work that they do together. Why is it that "the family that prays together stays together"?[1] It is because of the graces and blessings the Lord pours down on you and your family when you make Him the center of your lives. It is because of your growth in faith and your growth in love for God and for one another. And, it is because of the shared vulnerability, closeness, and trust created by family prayer. By praying together, your whole family learns to trust in and to rely on God and on each other. Each member of the family learns how to be there for the other members, just as God is there for each member of the family. A Monthly Family Meeting can be a cherished time of family togetherness, where you can pray together and in that context say very important things that you might not otherwise say.

Determine as a family a time for your Monthly Family Meeting. It can be Sunday after Mass, or a Friday or Saturday

---

[1] This maxim was written by Alfred J. Scalpone and popularized by Servant of God Father Patrick Peyton, C.S.C.

evening. You may also want to vote on a special dinner for that night to make the meeting something to look forward to even more.

This is a suggested Family Meeting format:

1. Gather together in the family room or another comfortable room.

2. Begin with praying aloud Psalm 23 (page 59) or with a prayer (either an Our Father or a spontaneous prayer, where Dad or Mom prays for God's blessings on the family and the family meeting in his or her own words).

3. Honor one another. Beginning either with the oldest or the youngest, take turns honoring one another, recognizing the goodness and the gifts in another family member present in the room. For instance, say you begin with the oldest. Dad begins by saying, "I would like to honor Mom and Sarah (second daughter). Granddad has been really sick and Mom and Sarah have been giving so much extra time to help Grandma take care of him. Double gold stars. Grandma is so grateful and happy because of you two." Then, when it gets down to one of the younger children, Brandon says, "I would like to honor Tim (older brother). I was having a hard time with my math homework, so Tim stopped what he was doing

and came to help me. He was really patient." When you honor one another, each person expresses gratitude for other members of the family, and the whole family begins to see and appreciate their own gifts and the gifts of others. All the members see that they are meant to be a gift and that they are meant to receive the gift that others are to them.

4. Ask forgiveness. Again beginning with either the oldest or the youngest, take turns asking forgiveness of one another. What is it that has happened in the past month that you regret? Whose forgiveness do you need? Each member of the family can apologize to one or more persons in the room. Especially in this step, parents can give a powerful example to their children. [It is important that no member of the family is ever disrespectful or accusatory of another member of the family. This destroys the intention of the Family Meeting. If one is hurt by another, one can share this respectfully in the next step.]

5. Share your life. In this step, going one by one in age order, the family members share with all the others:

   a. What is going on with them (their "status")—this can include things they struggle with or are upset about (work, school, sports, special events/ occurrences, etc.)

b. One great blessing received in the past month

c. One special intention that they would like the rest of the family to pray for

6. The Blessing. The father of the family then goes to each member and blesses each one (traces a Cross on their foreheads). He may choose to pray the blessing out loud and add other specific intentions for which he is asking the Lord on behalf of that member of the family (e.g., "Lord, please bless Jenny with your peace, and give her the wisdom she needs to make a decision about the next steps at school.").

7. Closing prayer. This can be either a Glory Be or a spontaneous prayer, in which Dad or Mom prays a thanksgiving in his or her own words.

By sharing your lives with each other in this way, you come to a deeper understanding of one another. You can see your common joys and your common struggles, and you can also better support one another and thank God for each other. After the Family Meeting is over, you can share a special dessert or have family games—this should be something interpersonal and interactive, not watching television or movies together; either a board game or a game outside where all can be involved, from the oldest to the youngest. Ending with something fun helps the whole family to look forward to the next Family Meeting even more.

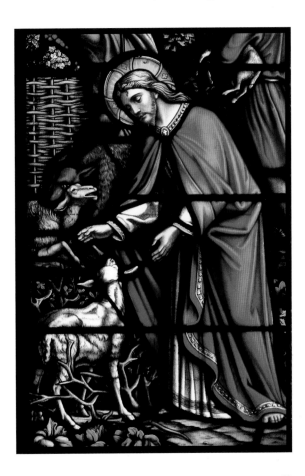

S · JOH· EII

· TA · ANNA

PRAYING WITH YOUR SPOUSE

That is why a man leaves his father and mother and clings to his wife, and the two of them become one body.

GENESIS 2:24

Husbands, love your wives, even as Christ loved the Church and handed himself over for her.

EPHESIANS 5:25

The love between you and your spouse and your love for God are the foundation and strength of your entire family. The stronger your love for one another and for God, the stronger your entire family is. Therefore, praying with your spouse is incredibly helpful and exceptionally powerful. Your spouse is the single most important person in your entire life. You can strengthen and support one another in the faith in a way no one else in the world can. Each of you has both the gift and the responsibility of helping your spouse and your children get to heaven.

The format for Praying with Your Spouse is similar to that of the Monthly Family Meeting, but it is more intimate, as it should be. It also includes a special time when you can pray together for your children. It would be ideal if you would pray with your spouse every night (perhaps immediately before going to bed) or at least once a week. You can sit together in your room or kneel down together at your bedside. If you prefer to pray in the morning, perhaps you could wake up 15 minutes earlier and pray together over a cup of coffee. Below is a suggested format for Praying with Your Spouse.

1. Place yourselves in the presence of God, conscious that side-by-side you approach Him. Then, give thanks to God for specific blessings of the (previous) day (or of the week) in your own words. You can do this together or take turns.

2. Honor one another (for anything that happened that day or week). Take turns doing this. (See Step 3 on page 61.)

3. Ask forgiveness of your spouse (for anything that happened that day or week). Take turns doing this. [It is important that neither spouse is ever accusatory or disrespectful of the other. If there is a grievance, hurt, or difficulty, it should be discussed with love and respect for the other.]

4. Share life. Share anything important or notable about your day or week with your spouse. Share your concerns and prayer intentions. Take turns doing this.

5. Intentions. Pray together (in your own words) for each one of your children. Going from oldest to youngest, ask for specific graces and blessings for each child.

6. Blessings. Bless one another, simply tracing a Cross on your spouse's forehead. Ask the Lord to give your spouse a particular grace and/or a specific blessing. Thank the Lord for the gift of your spouse.

7. Close with a Glory Be.

As you begin to pray with your spouse using this format, you will see that it takes more time some days and less time other days. It is always fruitful, and the Lord will bless you, your marriage, and your family each time you pray with your spouse.

If you would like to pray with your spouse in additional ways, consider reading the Sacred Scriptures together. For example, one of you can read the Gospel for the day to the other; then you can take turns sharing with each other the things that strike you about the passage and how it relates to your life. You might also make a resolution based on the passage; for instance, a resolution to try to be more patient, or to try to reach out to one particular child a little more, etc. You can use this same format (read, reflect, resolve) in reading a classic Catholic spiritual book together. You and your spouse may also pray the Rosary together for special family intentions.

[A] HOME IS . . . A PLACE OF AFFECTION, OF HELP, OF HOPE, OF SUPPORT.[1]

---

[1] Address of Pope Francis to Engaged Couples Preparing for Marriage; St. Peter's Square, February 14, 2014. © Libreria Editrice Vaticana 2014.

THE FAMILY ROSARY

THE APOSTLES' CREED

I believe in God, the Father Almighty,
Creator of heaven and earth;
and in Jesus Christ, His only Son Our Lord,
who was conceived by the Holy Spirit, born
of the Virgin Mary,
suffered under Pontius Pilate,
was crucified, died, and was buried.
He descended into hell; the third day He rose
again from the dead;
He ascended into heaven,
and is seated at the right hand of God,
the Father Almighty;
from thence He shall come to judge
the living and the dead.
I believe in the Holy Spirit,
the holy Catholic Church,
the communion of saints,
the forgiveness of sins,
the resurrection of the body,
and life everlasting.
Amen.

passage
by pra
"℞." (
passa

2. Proc
℣.

℞

T
℣

℞. I believe in the

The Announcement of the Mysteries

℣. The Five _____ _____ (Joyful, Luminous, Sorrowful, or Glorious) Mysteries

THE DECADES

[Select the mysteries you would like to pray. Use this structure for each of the five (5) decades.]

The Announcement of the Decade

℣. The ___ (1st, 2nd, 3rd, 4th, or 5th) ___ (Joyful, Luminous, Sorrowful, or Glorious) Mystery, the ___ (For example: The first decade is the Annunciation, The Baptism of Our Lord, the Agony in the Garden, or the Resurrection, depending on the mysteries you have chosen to pray).

The Our Father

℣. Our Father, who art in heaven, hallowed be Thy name. Thy kingdom come. Thy will be done, on earth as it is in heaven.

℞ Give us this day our daily bread, and forgive us our trespasses, as we forgive those who trespass against us. And lead us not into temptation, but deliver us from evil. Amen.

Ten (10) Hail Marys
[During each of these Hail Marys, all are invited to think about the mystery announced.]

℣. Hail Mary, full of grace, the Lord is with thee. Blessed art thou among women, and blessed is the fruit of thy womb, Jesus.
℞. Holy Mary, Mother of God, pray for us sinners now and at the hour of our death. Amen.

[Pray the Hail Mary as above a total of ten (10) times.]

The Glory Be
℣. Glory be to the Father, and to the Son, and to the Holy Spirit.
℞. As it was in the beginning, is now and ever shall be, world without end. Amen.

After the five decades are completed:

The Hail Holy Queen

℣. Hail, holy Queen,

℟. Mother of mercy, our life, our sweetness, and our hope. To thee do we cry, poor banished children of Eve. To thee do we send up our sighs, mourning and weeping in this valley of tears. Turn, then, most gracious advocate, thine eyes of mercy toward us, and after this, our exile, show unto us the blessed fruit of thy womb, Jesus. O clement, O loving, O sweet Virgin Mary.

℣. Pray for us, O holy Mother of God.

℟. That we may be made worthy of the promises of Christ.

Concluding Prayer

℣. Let us pray. O God,

℟. whose Only-Begotten Son, by His life, death, and resurrection, has purchased for us the rewards of eternal life, grant, we beseech Thee, that meditating upon these mysteries of the most holy Rosary of the Blessed Virgin Mary, we may imitate what they contain, and obtain what they promise, through the same Christ Our Lord. Amen.

℣. May the divine assistance remain always with us.

℟. And may the souls of the faithful departed, through the mercy of God, rest in peace. Amen.

℣. In the name of the Father, and of the Son, and of the Holy Spirit.

℟. Amen.

You may want to obtain Rosary meditation booklets for you and your children to use during the Family Rosary. You can even let your children pick out their own Rosary meditation books.

By praying the Rosary together as a family, you live concretely the faith you all share, the faith you want your children to receive so that it becomes a part of them. One of the best times to pray the Family Rosary might be after dinner, after all the dishes have been washed and the leftovers have been put away. It can be a sacred time of family togetherness when you, as a family, pray and think about the life of Jesus.

Moreover, in giving the Rosary this prime time, you give faith and family priority over everything else in your life, whether it be entertainment, work, or relaxation. Some families also choose to have dinner and the Family Rosary mark the beginning of the "black out," the time when all use of television, computers, cell phones, and electronic devices comes to an end for the day so that the family members can be present to one another and to the Lord.

Although the Family Rosary (one set of five decades) only takes about 15 to 20 minutes, it can be a challenge, especially in families with younger children. Do not let this discourage you. Younger children can still be present and listen quietly to the prayers, even as they play, etc., during the Family Rosary. As the children grow older, they can take turns leading a decade of the Rosary. Lighting candles around the sacred images where you pray the Rosary can be helpful in creating an atmosphere of prayer. You can all sit in a particular area to say the Family Rosary and/or have the option of kneeling. You can choose to say a Family Rosary every night or choose one or more particular nights on which you will pray it together. If you are traveling, have a long commute, or are in traffic, the Rosary is a wonderful prayer to pray for your family and for other special intentions. If you would like, you can begin by simply praying one decade every day, praying perhaps a different mystery every day on the way to school or after dinner clean-up. You might allow the children to choose the mystery and lead it.

PHASE THREE

ADVANCING IN THE LIFE OF PRAYER

Prayer Outside the Home
Angel of God
Prayer to St. Michael
Prayer Before Sporting Events

Preparing for the Sacraments
Preparing for Mass as a Family
Going to Confession as a Family
Thanksgiving After Holy Communion
Using Holy Water and Other Sacramentals

ANGEL OF GOD

Angel of God,
my guardian dear,
to whom His love commits me here,
ever this day be at my side,
to light and guard,
to rule and guide.
Amen.

This beloved prayer has been a part of the Christian life for centuries. Dating back to the Middle Ages, this prayer serves as a daily invocation of the special angel God has given to each one of us, a Guardian Angel. If we allow them, Guardian Angels protect us from evil spirits and help us to avoid sin. They can also help us know what to do in order to fulfill God's will. These beautiful angels of ours constantly behold the face of God (cf. Mt 18:10).

Since angels guard us and keep us safe on journeys, it is a custom to pray the Angel of God prayer when you get in the car to go somewhere (whether alone or as a family). Many families use it as their "driving prayer" and pray it together in the car. As with all other prayers, it begins and ends with the Sign of the Cross. You can also say this prayer as soon as you wake up in the morning. You can pray it at other times throughout the day if you would like, especially when you need the help of your Guardian Angel. Remind your children that their Guardian Angels love them and want them to get to heaven, so they should ask their Guardian Angels to protect them when they are afraid and to help them when they are tempted to do wrong. Hopefully, at the end of our lives, our Guardian Angels will welcome us into heaven. There we can thank them face to face.

PRAYER TO ST. MICHAEL

Saint Michael the Archangel,
defend us in battle.
Be our protection against
the wickedness and snares of the devil.
May God rebuke him, we humbly pray;
and do thou, O Prince of the Heavenly Host,
by the power of God,
cast into hell Satan
and all the evil spirits
who prowl about the world
seeking the ruin of souls.
Amen.

Be sober and vigilant. Your opponent the devil is prowling around like a roaring lion looking for [someone] to devour. Resist him, steadfast in faith, knowing that your fellow believers throughout the world undergo the same sufferings (1 Pt 5:8-9).

For our struggle is not with flesh and blood but with the principalities, with the powers, with the world rulers of this present darkness, with the evil spirits in the heavens (Eph 6:12).

Understanding and experiencing the evil forces of Satan, Pope Leo XIII (Pope from 1878 to 1903) composed the Prayer to St. Michael and asked the faithful to pray it after the Holy Sacrifice of the Mass. Although this practice is no longer actively in place everywhere in the Universal Church, many Catholics are accustomed to call upon the help of St. Michael each day and especially in times of temptation and difficulty.

In the great heavenly battle between the devils and the angels, it was St. Michael who led the conquest of Satan and his followers (cf. Rev 12:7-9). His name captures his mission: "Michael" means "Who is like God?" It was precisely the power and authority of God that the devils questioned and rejected, for they wanted to be like God. Yet Michael proves to them that no creature is like God, no created being is equal to God. With courage, wisdom, and humility, Michael led the battle against Satan and prevailed. For this reason, Michael is called the "Prince of the Heavenly Hosts," meaning he is the "Prince of the Heavenly Armies."

From now until the end of time, Satan and his devils (demons or evil spirits) "prowl about the world seeking the ruin of souls"—that is, they seek to tempt us and lead us into sin, presenting us with evil thoughts and evil desires, luring us to go to evil places and/or to do wicked things. The devils are known for their subtlety, for they not only try to prevent or distract us from doing good things (such as praying as a family, performing works of service, going to Mass, etc.), but they also lure us into sin gradually; for instance, by beginning to tempt us through boredom and indifference, then leading us to pride, gossip, or self-centered day-dreaming, and then to more serious sins. The devils want as many souls in hell as possible. It is because Satan and his devils are so clever and so unrelenting that we ask St. Michael to protect and defend us each day. Of course, our Guardian Angels also help us. By His Cross, Christ has conquered Satan. Jesus is infinitely more powerful than all the demons together. Close to Him, we have no need to be afraid!

Praying the Prayer to St. Michael together is a good way to start your day. You might choose to say it right after the Grace After Meals at breakfast, at the front door before everyone goes in different directions, or in the car together as you head to school. Some pray it following the Family Rosary; others pray it before going to bed at night. You can determine the time that is best for your family to pray this prayer.

PRAYER BEFORE SPORTING EVENTS

Strong and faithful God,
as we come together for this contest,
we ask you to bless these athletes.

Keep them safe from injury and harm,
instill in them respect for each other, and
reward them for their
perseverance.

Lead us all to the rewards of your kingdom
where you live and reign for
ever and ever.
Amen.[1]

---

[1] Excerpt from the *Book of Blessings*, additional blessings for use in the United States of America © 1988 United States Conference of Catholic Bishops, Washington, DC. Used with permission. All rights reserved.

Participating in sports can be a grace-filled opportunity for your children to learn and practice the virtues of sportsmanship, such as perseverance, attentiveness to others, concentration, discipline, courage, fair-play, justice, friendship, and solidarity. Sports can also build your children's sense of community—of working together toward a common goal—as well as a sense of pride and loyalty to the team and the ideals the team represents. Learning both to win and to lose graciously prepares your children for life, where both victories and defeats are encountered continually. They see that getting up again after a fall is as important as not becoming arrogant after a victory.

In fact, sports can help children to understand the Christian life better. St. Paul compares the Christian life to a race:

> Do you not know that the runners in the stadium all run in the race, but only one wins the prize? Run so as to win. Every athlete exercises discipline in every way. They do it to win a perishable crown, but we, an imperishable one (1 Cor 9:24-25).

Just as athletes discipline and exert themselves for an earthly victory, we must discipline and exert ourselves for the heavenly victory. Just as running, hitting, and kicking must be learned in sports, so prayer, self-giving, and forgiveness must be learned in the Christian life. Oftentimes, you can teach your children spiritual lessons through what they experience in playing sports. Encourage them to turn to the Lord for strength and wisdom.

You can pray the Prayer Before Sporting Events in the car, on the way to the game. Begin and end the prayer with the Sign of the Cross.

Saint Sebastian is the patron saint of athletes and soldiers.

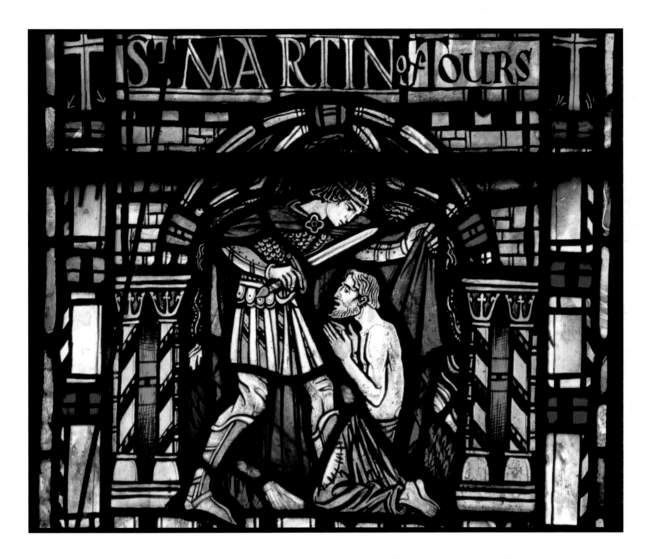

St. Martin of Tours, depicted in this window, is a famous soldier-saint of the 4th Century. Seeing a beggar on a cold day, Martin took out his sword and cut his military cloak in half; then, he wrapped the half-cloak around the beggar. Later that evening, Jesus Christ Himself appeared wearing the same half-cloak. He thanked Martin, most likely with words similar to those we find in the Gospel of St. Matthew: "Come, blessed of My Father . . . for I was naked and you clothed Me" (cf. Mt 25:34-36).

PREPARING FOR MASS AS A FAMILY

[Jesus Christ], because he remains forever,
has a priesthood
that does not pass away.
Therefore, he is always able
to save those
who approach God through him,
since he lives forever
to make intercession for them.
It was fitting
that we should have such a high priest:
holy, innocent, undefiled,
separated from sinners,
higher than the heavens.
He has no need,
as did the high priests,
to offer sacrifice day after day,
first for his own sins
and then for those of the people;
he did that once for all
when he offered himself [on the Cross].

HEBREWS 7:24-27

ice, slander, and obscene language out of your mouths. Stop lying to one another, since you have taken off the old self with its practices and have put on the new self, which is being renewed, for knowledge, in the image of its creator. . . . Put on then, as God's chosen ones, holy and beloved, heartfelt compassion, kindness, humility, gentleness, and patience, bearing with one another and forgiving one another, if one has a grievance against another; as the Lord has forgiven you, so must you also do. And over all these virtues put on love, that is, the bond of perfection. And let the peace of Christ control your hearts, the peace into which you were also called in one body. And be thankful. Let the word of Christ dwell in you richly, as in all wisdom you teach and admonish one another, singing psalms, hymns, and spiritual songs with gratitude in your hearts to God. And whatever you do, in word or in deed, do everything in the name of the Lord Jesus, giving thanks to God the Father through him (Col 3:5-10, 12-17).

The more we can live the Word of God that we read in Scripture, the better prepared we are to receive Jesus, who is The Word of God, in the Eucharist. The more we receive Jesus in the Eucharist, the more grace we will have to live out the Word of God and to live like Jesus, the Word of God. At Mass, Christ is present to us at the "Table of His Word" (in the Scriptures) and in the "Table of His Body" (in Holy Communion). The readings at Mass are the way that God speaks to us and prepares our hearts to receive Him more fully in the Eucharist. A good way to prepare for Mass is by reading the readings for the day before we go.

One way your family can prepare for Mass is by using the following format:

1. Choose a person to be responsible for finding and bringing one of the Scripture passages that will be read at Mass on the coming Sunday. It is simplest to begin with the Gospel reading, or you may even choose to begin with the Scripture passage quoted above.

2. At the time you choose as a family (Saturday afternoon or evening, or perhaps Sunday after breakfast but before Mass), sit down together and make the Sign of the Cross. Then, one family member reads the Scripture passage aloud. Meanwhile, everyone else listens.

3. One parent can go first in sharing a word, a sentence, or a striking idea, explaining why they liked it or what it made them think of. They can give examples or tell a related

story. They could also share a specific way they hear the Gospel calling them to change for the better. Here, Mom's or Dad's example will speak volumes to the children.

4. The parent could ask the children what they noticed or what stood out for them. Often, to take the conversation deeper, a good follow-up question to a comment may be one (or more) of the following: "Why do you think that is so?"; "How does that apply to us?"; "Have you ever been in that kind of situation?"; "Why do you think that person responded that way?"; and, "What is one thing that we could do today to practice that?" As your family becomes more comfortable sharing in this way, you could change the expectation from voluntary response to every person contributing something. It is best to be careful and gentle with this, however, because you don't want your children or your spouse to develop a distaste for prayer.

5. You can close the preparation time by thanking each other and the Lord, remembering that the word "Eucharist" means "thanksgiving." End by praying together a Glory Be.

6. Thank everyone for this time together.

This way of preparing for Mass takes advantage of the fact that family members have a grace to teach each other and help each other (with gentleness) to grow in holiness. By sharing the Scriptures together, you will find yourselves growing closer to one another

and understanding one another better. You will begin to love each other more through this shared openness and vulnerability. You will begin to love Our Lord more as well. It is important to emphasize gentleness both with oneself and with others. Preparing for Mass as a family should never turn into a time of arguing, accusing, or faultfinding; rather, it is a time to experience the whole family's shared desire for God and for holiness.

If the above is too difficult given your current family situation, an alternative is to try to do this preparation in the car on the way to Mass. Another time-reducing strategy (for those who have large families) would be to take turns sharing each week. For instance, four members take responsibility for sharing this week; next week, four different members take responsibility for sharing.

On the way home from Mass, instead of turning on the music or plugging into devices, you may ask if anyone noticed something different in the readings or remembered anything special from the homily to share. Knowing the family is going to discuss the readings and the homily on the way home is a help to being attentive during Mass. As parents, talking about the faith and the way that it affects everyday situations and decisions is an

invaluable tool in helping to form the way our children think about the world and integrate their faith into their everyday lives.

HOW TO LOOK UP A SCRIPTURE PASSAGE

Scripture references are most often given in this format: Jn 3:16. The first set of letters indicates the Book of the Bible to which the passage belongs. The first number indicates the chapter number. The second number (the number after the colon) indicates the verse number.

In this case, "Jn" stands for "John," the Gospel of John. Checking the table of contents in your Bible, you can go to the section of your Bible that has the Gospel of John.

Next is the "3." This first number indicates the chapter of the book. Go to Chapter 3 of John's Gospel.

Finally, you will notice that each line or verse in that chapter has a number. You are looking for verse "16."

This should be the verse that you find: "For God so loved the world that he gave his only Son, so that everyone who believes in him might not perish but might have eternal life" (Jn 3:16).

Look over the table of contents in the Bible. This will help you to become more familiar with the names of the books of the Bible and their abbreviations. So, for instance, when you see "1 Cor 2:9," you will know that is the First Letter of St. Paul to the Corinthians, and when you see "2 Thes 3:9," you will know that it is the Second Letter of St. Paul to the Thessalonians. Study especially the Old Testament books, so that when you see "Mal 1:11," you will know it is the Book of the Prophet Malachi; and, when you see "2 Mc 12:39-45," you will know it is the Second Book of Maccabees, Chapter 12, verses 39 to 45.

The more often you look up Scripture passages, the better you will become at doing it. It is a wonderful thing to have a personal copy of the Bible, one that becomes more and more worn with time as you grow closer to the Lord. If you prefer to use an app, try the New American Bible app.

May the Lord's Word continually give joy to your hearts!

GOING TO MASS AS A FAMILY

Arriving a little early for Mass can give you and your family extra time to get ready for Mass. Sit where your children can see what is going on.

You can teach your children how to make a habit of blessing themselves with holy water, dipping the right hand in the holy water and then making the Sign of the Cross. This is a reminder of our Baptism.

You can also teach them the habit of genuflecting when passing directly in front of the tabernacle (the special place in which the Blessed Sacrament is reserved, usually marked by a sanctuary lamp, a lighted candle hanging from the ceiling or on a stand) and genuflecting toward the tabernacle before they enter the pew or row of seats. When you genuflect, you simply touch your right knee to the ground. Other gestures sometimes accompanying the genuflection are a head bow and the Sign of the Cross. We genuflect to recognize the presence of Our Lord in the Blessed Sacrament within the tabernacle. We humble ourselves before Our Lord, the King of Kings.

Once you are in your seats, and if there is time before Mass begins, pray three Hail Marys together quietly, asking Our Blessed Mother to prepare your hearts for receiving Our Lord in

His Word (the readings and homily) and in His Body (the Eucharist, or Holy Communion).

If you have infants and toddlers who are apt to become restless during Mass, consider alternating Sundays with your spouse for taking the little one out of Mass for fresh air, so that it is not always the same parent missing parts of the Liturgy.

Stay for a few minutes after Mass to pray together in thanksgiving for the Mass and for the whole week. You can pray in your own words, or pray the Glory Be three times. That simple prayer of praise gives Him glory. It also draws you to contemplate His presence with and within you. Be in His presence. Be with Him whom you have just received.

GOING TO CONFESSION AS A FAMILY

THE ACT OF CONTRITION

O my God,
I am heartily sorry for having offended Thee,
and I detest all my sins
because of Thy just punishments,
but most of all because
they offend Thee, my God,
who art all good and deserving of all my love.
I firmly resolve
with the help of Thy grace
to sin no more and
to avoid the near occasion of sin.
Amen.[1]

---

[1] From the *Compendium of the Catechism of the Catholic Church*, Appendix A. English translation copyright © 2006 Libreria Editrice Vaticana. All rights reserved. Used with permission of the United States Conference of the Catholic Bishops, Washington, D.C.

In the early days of Christianity, people were moved by the followers of Christ: "See," they said, "how these Christians love one another!" What is at the heart of this love which Christians have for one another? What is it that frees them to live their everyday lives so full of love? Forgiveness. Christians know the joy of being forgiven by their loving Father. Forgiveness is one of the most sincere and most genuine expressions of love. As Jesus was dying on the Cross, He was praying to God the Father for the men who called for His crucifixion and the men who nailed Him to the Cross. Jesus said, "Father, forgive them, they know not what they do" (Lk 23:34). With these words, Jesus was also praying for us. Forgiveness is the great gift that Jesus won for us on the Cross, for it is on the Cross that He suffered and died for our sins. He took upon Himself the burden of our sins in order to set us free from our guilt and reconcile us to our loving Father. Jesus did this because He loves us.

By going to the sacrament of Confession (also called Reconciliation or Penance), we acknowledge and accept this marvelous gift of forgiveness, and we allow all that Jesus did for us on the Cross to be applied to our souls individually and specifically. Going to Confession is an act of faith and an act of worship. By going to Confession we say to God, "You are God; You can forgive my sins. You can heal me. I'm sorry for my sins. Please forgive me. Help me to change my life and stop sinning. Please take me back and bring me close to you again."

Help your children to remember that when we go to Confession we are running back to the embrace of the Lord, who has been waiting for us. He loves us. There is no sin we could ever commit that would cause Him to stop loving us. There is no sin that He cannot forgive except the sin(s) we will not allow Him to forgive. He wants to forgive us. He wants to be close to us. He doesn't want us to remain in our sins and suffer the loneliness and pain they cause us.

Going to Confession helps us grow closer not only to God but also to one another, because receiving God's forgiveness makes it easier for us to forgive each other. This is the reason Jesus taught us to pray in the Our Father, "forgive us our trespasses [sins/wrongdoings] as we forgive those who trespass against us [who do wrong to us]" Just as we ask God to forgive us, we give forgiveness to those who have hurt us. Jesus forgives us. Jesus died for our sins because He loves us, so we accept little "deaths"—that is, hurts and pain—caused by other people's sins against us. Together with Jesus, we forgive them out of love. Receiving God's forgiveness gives us the strength and the grace to forgive others. The sacrament of Confession also gives us special graces, namely the grace to be sorry for our sins and the grace to love God as He deserves to be loved.

Although the Church asks us to go to Confession at least once a year, it is a very worthwhile practice to go to Confession as a family once a month. Sometimes, choosing a particular Saturday of the month makes it easier to remember to go to Confession as part of your family schedule. For example, every first Saturday of the month, the whole family goes to Confession. Once you decide on a time you will all go to Confession together, each member then knows to expect it and to plan on it. If monthly confession is something your family should ease into, consider going to Confession together once every two months for a while until your family is ready to go to Confession every month. If you have older children, ask them to research times and places for Confession, and allow them to suggest good times and places for the family to go to Confession together. Allowing them the opportunity to contribute in this way will help them to be more active participants.

In terms of preparing for Confession, there are several ways you might do this as a family. One suggestion is offered here, but you may find another way that better suits your family.

Before the actual family gathering to prepare for Confession together, parents should choose an appropriate Examination of Conscience[2] (a list of questions that helps you

---

[2] For a recommended Examination of Conscience, visit http://www.usccb.org/prayer-and-worship/sacra- ments-and-sacramentals/penance/examinations-of- conscience.cfm.

One of the scribes . . . asked [Jesus], "Which is the first of all the commandments?" Jesus replied, "The first is this: 'Hear, O Israel! The Lord our God is Lord alone! You shall love the Lord your God with all your heart, with all your soul, with all your mind, and with all your strength.' The second is this: 'You shall love your neighbor as yourself.' There is no other commandment greater than these."

MARK 12:28-31

to think about and remember sins you may have committed since your last Confession). Depending on the age range and developmental stages of your children, you may want to have more than one type of Examination of Conscience. There are many good examinations for both teens and younger children. Obtain a hard copy of the Examination of Conscience you have chosen to use. Highlight the questions you would like read aloud to your children. Bring this copy to the family preparation gathering. If you would like to begin with something more simple, you may use the Ten Commandments (on page 107) as your Examination of Conscience.

At the gathering (either before leaving for the church or the evening before), you may do the following:

1. Open by praying an Our Father together. Then, read aloud Mark 12:28-31.

2. Make an examination of conscience together. Have one person slowly read aloud each of the (highlighted) questions on the Examination of Conscience, pausing a little after each question. The silent pause allows each person to answer the question before the Lord. (No one should answer the questions aloud or accuse another person.)

If the Examination of Conscience is fairly long, then have the children take turns reading the questions aloud. For instance, one child can read five questions, then pass it to the next child who also reads five questions, etc. Remind the children that if they have questions about how to go to Confession, they can ask you, or they can ask the priest once they are inside the confessional.

When you arrive at the church, each person old enough can go to Confession. It is a wonderful example for the parents to go to Confession first.

After your family has gone to Confession—and all the members have had an opportunity to say their penance—you may all kneel down together and say a Glory Be in thanksgiving for the gift of forgiveness, for Jesus' Death and Resurrection. Then, your whole family could go out and do something fun, or go home and have some ice cream.

Celebrating the Lord's mercy and forgiveness is important. It helps your children to see that we have far more reasons for joy than anything else! And by celebrating God's mercy and love, we begin to experience here on earth a little bit of what heaven is like.

THE TEN COMMANDMENTS[3]

1. I am the LORD your God: you shall not have strange gods before me.

2. You shall not take the name of the LORD your God in vain.

3. Remember to keep holy the LORD's Day.

4. Honor your father and your mother.

5. You shall not kill.

6. You shall not commit adultery.

7. You shall not steal.

8. You shall not bear false witness against your neighbor.

9. You shall not covet your neighbor's wife.

10. You shall not covet your neighbor's goods.

[3] Traditional Catechetical Formula of the Ten Commandments as found in the *Catechism of the Catholic Church, Part III.*

THANKSGIVING AFTER HOLY COMMUNION

ANIMA CHRISTI ("SOUL OF CHRIST")

Soul of Christ, sanctify me.
Body of Christ, save me.
Blood of Christ, inebriate me.
Water from the side of Christ, wash me.
Passion of Christ, strengthen me.
O good Jesus, hear me.
Within Your wounds, hide me.
Suffer me not to be separated from You.
From the malicious enemy defend me.
In the hour of my death, call me
and bid me come unto You
that with Your saints I may praise You
forever and ever.
Amen.[1]

---

[1] Dating back to 1370 (*The Catholic Encyclopedia*, s.v. "Anima Christi"), this revered prayer unites meditation and petition.

The moment after we have received Holy Communion is a time of supreme closeness to God. The God of the universe, the Creator of all things, who cannot be contained or limited to any one place or time, comes to rest in our hearts.

One image that can help us to understand this mystery of God dwelling within us after Holy Communion is the image of the burning bush in Exodus 3:2, "although the bush was on fire, it was not being consumed." After we have received Our Lord in Holy Communion, we are like that burning bush—the power, light, beauty, heat, and strength of the fire represent the presence and the glory of God Himself. The bush represents us. Simple, humble, ordinary. The bush is not consumed; it is not destroyed by the fire but holds the fire, reveals the fire. In the same way, we are not consumed or destroyed by the presence of God within us after Holy Communion. Rather, we are given the grace to reveal God to others by our love, our kindness, our generosity, and our goodness to others.

Thus, praying together as a family a special Thanksgiving After Holy Communion can be exceptionally powerful. One way of praying a thanksgiving prayer together is to remain in the church and wait until the other people have left. When there are relatively few people left in the church, you can kneel as a family and pray one of these prayers together. You might also have some minutes of silence afterwards, during which you and your children can give thanks to God for the gift of Himself in the Eucharist. Remind your children that this is truly a very, very special time with God. They will come to treasure it more and more, as will you.

A THANKSGIVING
AFTER
HOLY COMMUNION

O Sacrament most holy,
O Sacrament divine,
all praise and all thanksgiving,
be every moment Thine.
O Jesus, I love You in the Eucharist;
a hundred thousand welcomes,
a hundred thousand thanks.
Unworthy as I am, make me better,
better able to know Thee,
to love Thee, to serve Thee,
to accept and do Thy will in all things.
Glory be to the Father, and to the Son,
and to the Holy Spirit,
as it was in the beginning, is now and ever
shall be, world without end. Amen.[2]

---

[2] This prayer was compiled by Father Patrick Magnier, C.Ss.R., a member of the Baltimore Province of the Redemptorists, who had a great devotion to the Blessed Sacrament. It is republished here with permission.

USING HOLY WATER AND OTHER SACRAMENTALS

What was from the beginning,
what we have heard,
what we have seen with our eyes,
what we looked upon
and touched with our hands
concerns the Word of life—
for the life was made visible . . .
[in] Jesus Christ.

CF. 1 JOHN 1:1-3

Sacramentals are sacred signs
instituted by the Church.
They prepare [us] to receive
the fruit of the sacraments and
sanctify different circumstances of life.[1]

---
[1] *Catechism of the Catholic Church*, 1677.

God became incarnate, taking on a human body and soul like ours in order to draw us into the mystery and truth of God. Now, He continues to work through things that we can see, hear, touch, taste, and smell to save us and make us holy. The seven sacraments are the best example of this. For example, in Baptism we see and feel the water that truly cleanses us from sin, taking away the stain of original sin and also taking away any personal sin we may have at that moment. Since we cannot receive all the sacraments on a regular basis, the Lord has given us a means by which we can be more prepared for the grace of the sacraments and more likely to cooperate with that grace: the sacramentals.

Sacramentals are sacred signs. One of the most important types of sacramentals is a ceremony of blessing. An example of a ceremony of blessing is the Grace Before and After Meals that you already use as a family. It praises God and thanks Him for His gifts. Other ceremonies of blessing have led to Catholics possessing many blessed objects, such as crucifixes, rosaries, medals, scapulars, palm branches, and sacred images. It is a popular practice to call these blessed objects "sacramentals," though technically it is the ceremony of blessing that is the sacramental. For simplicity's sake, we will use the word "sacramental" in its popular sense.

Holy water is a sacramental that helps us to remember the graces of our Baptism. If we use it with reverence and attention, blessing ourselves with it in our homes, it can help us to be open to the grace God wishes to give us. Having a holy water font in your home is a beautiful gift to your family. Your children can take turns filling the family holy water font. They can also takes turns bringing the empty holy water bottles to church on Sunday to be refilled. You can put your family holy water font by the front door or by the door through which your family members most frequently go in and out. If needed, you can have several holy water fonts. Hopefully you can form the habit of blessing yourselves with holy water as you go in and out of your home, for your home is now a sacred space, a special place of love and prayer, a place filled with the presence of God.

A noteworthy practice of Catholics through the ages is that of house blessings, especially during the Easter Season. You can invite a priest to come and bless your family and every room in your home, dedicating it to the Lord and inviting Him to be the center of your home and family life. This ceremony can be preceded or followed by a family dinner together with the priest. This tradition also affords your children the opportunity to see a priest in their own home and to grow in reverence for the priesthood.

In a way similar to holy water, the other sacramentals (e.g., crucifixes, rosaries, medals, scapulars, and sacred images) also help to open our minds and hearts by appealing to our senses. For example, a crucifix can help a teenager to see what Jesus' face looked like as He was dying on the Cross. The teen sees also the wounds in His hands and His feet, as well as His crown of thorns. Seeing this, the teen can begin to understand interiorly the depth of Jesus' love for us. Having other sacred images in your home, such as icons, an image of Our Lady of Guadalupe, the Divine Mercy, or the Holy Family, can turn your minds and hearts to the things of heaven. Children can be comforted by seeing a Guardian Angel nightlight or an illuminated statue of the Blessed Virgin Mary in the hallway. Wearing a Miraculous Medal or a scapular is like placing Mary over our hearts, entrusting our heart to her and receiving her special protection.

Sacramentals help to open us to receive and cooperate with grace, that is, to receive and cooperate with God's presence and goodness at work in our daily lives.

PHASE FOUR

THE POWER OF PRAYER

INTERCESSORY PRAYER

First of all, then, I ask that supplications,
prayers, petitions, and thanksgivings
be offered for everyone. . . .
that we may lead a quiet and tranquil life
in all devotion and dignity.
This is good and pleasing to God our savior,
who wills everyone to be saved
and to come to
knowledge of the truth.

1 TIMOTHY 2:1-4

Intercessory prayer is simple. It can consist of just stating a petition (what you are asking for): "For the hurricane victims to receive the help they need." After the petition, you may also add one Our Father, one Hail Mary, and one Glory Be, if you would like.

Intercessory prayer helps us to think of others and to avoid an unhealthy preoccupation with ourselves.

There are additional ways to foster intercessory prayer and to help your children to grow in faith and trust. For example, you could have a special bulletin board in your home dedicated to special prayer intentions. The first intentions on your family prayer board could be these:

1. For the Holy Father and his intentions
2. For the Church throughout the world
3. For our country and government leaders
4. For the souls in Purgatory
5. For members of your family and your extended family (you can make these more specific)

Whenever a child or parent has a special prayer intention, either the child or a parent may write the intention on a small slip of paper and post it on the bulletin board. This way, every family member can see and pray for each other's intentions. At a particular time every day, the whole family can pray for all these intentions. An easy time to do this is at the Grace After Meals. After the words, "May the souls of the faithful departed . . . rest in peace," simply add the line: "and for all the intentions on our prayer board." The family members reply, "Amen," and you close with the Sign of the Cross. Or, if you prefer, you can pray for these intentions at the beginning of the Family Rosary or at the conclusion of the Family Bedtime Prayers.

"EXTRA SPECIAL" INTENTIONS

Sometimes, you or your children may have "extra special" intentions (very personal and important intentions). For these cases, you may use another Catholic tradition: write the name of the person you are praying for or the intention you are praying for on a slip of paper. (You can write "extra special intention" if you prefer not to write the actual intention.)

Then, place this slip of paper underneath a statue of Our Lord, the Blessed Virgin Mary, Saint Joseph, or another saint. This symbolizes that you entrust your petition to Our Lord, the Blessed Virgin Mary, Saint Joseph, or another saint, and ask them to also pray with you for this "extra special" intention. The saints are our friends and they want to pray with us.

OFFERING SACRIFICES

I urge you therefore, brothers,
by the mercies of God,
to offer your bodies as a living sacrifice,
holy and pleasing to God,
your spiritual worship.
Do not conform yourselves to this age
but be transformed
by the renewal of your mind,
that you may discern what is the will of God,
what is good and pleasing and perfect.

ROMANS 12:1-2

injured in a car accident—you can make your prayer for them through sacrifices, such as giving up desserts for three days, not watching television or using electronic devices, or staying home to help with housework instead of going to the mall. These forms of "self-denial" are sacrifices, and these sacrifices are prayers that, united with Jesus' sacrifice of Himself on the Cross, can win many graces for others, including healing, strength, and comfort.

Through our sacrifices, we can also help to make reparation for our own sins and the sins of others. "Making reparation" means repairing the damage caused by sin, or making up, through loving deeds such as prayer and sacrifice, for the offense given to God. This is analogous to the way a man who somehow offends his wife in the morning will bring flowers to her in the evening to make "reparation" for the offense. The most perfect act of reparation was Jesus' suffering and death. This is why going to Mass is so important. When we make reparation, we unite our prayers and sacrifices to Jesus' perfect sacrifice of Himself on the Cross.

In addition to choosing sacrifices of our own to make, we can also choose to offer as sacrifices other sufferings that come our way. These sacrifices may be an even better form of prayer, precisely because we don't choose for these difficult or sad things to happen to us, but

A very powerful form of intercessory prayer is to offer sacrifices for particular people or particular intentions. By offering sacrifices, you pray not only with your spirit but also with your body. So, if you or your family has a special intention—for instance, your next door neighbor who has just been diagnosed with cancer, or a teenager who has been seriously

they do happen to us, such as when another person mistreats us or when the weather causes the cancellation of a game we were happily anticipating. These sufferings are a part of life, but instead of turning in on ourselves with sadness, we can turn toward serving the needs of others by making that unpleasant thing a prayer in the form of a sacrifice. This means that we offer an unpleasant or disappointing occurrence together with Christ to the Father for the salvation of souls, or to make reparation for our own sins or the sins of others.

Children readily accept this practice of offering sufferings as sacrifices. Once it is explained to them, it becomes a wonderful way of transforming disappointing things into opportunities for good. For instance, your son may have fallen or been pushed by another child, resulting in a scraped knee. Hopefully, the child informed the adult supervising at the time; however, he may still be upset. By helping your child to think about Jesus when He was pushed by the soldiers as He was carrying His Cross, and how He fell and bruised His knees, you make it clear that the child can be united to Jesus in this small way. Instead of choosing to hate those who were mistreating Him, Jesus chose to forgive them and to love them. Your child can do the same. Your child can offer his

pain, both physical and spiritual, as a sacrifice for the person who hurt him or for another special intention (such as for a sick sibling or for a woman in the parish who has just lost her husband, etc.) By offering sacrifices, we learn to look beyond our own suffering to the suffering of Christ and others. United with Christ, we offer our suffering as a gift, a prayer, a sacrifice, that will help others in their needs and difficulties.

THE DIVINE MERCY CHAPLET

℣. You expired, Jesus, but the source of life gushed forth for souls, and the ocean of mercy opened up for the whole world. O Fount of Life, unfathomable Divine Mercy, envelop the whole world and empty Yourself out upon us.

℣. O Blood and Water, which gushed forth from the Heart of Jesus as a fountain of Mercy for us,

℞. I trust in You!

℣. O Blood and Water, which gushed forth from the Heart of Jesus as a fountain of Mercy for us,

℞. I trust in You!

℣. O Blood and Water, which gushed forth from the Heart of Jesus as a fountain of Mercy for us,

℞. I trust in You![1]

---

[1] This text and the text of the prayers on the following pages in this section are taken from the *Diary of St. Maria Faustina Kowalska: Divine Mercy in My Soul* © 1987 Marian Fathers of the Immaculate Conception of the B.V.M. All rights reserved. Used with permission.

Another prayer which the family may use to foster devotion is the Divine Mercy Chaplet. This special "chaplet" (a series of prayers usually prayed on a set of beads) may be prayed on a set of rosary beads.

The Divine Mercy Chaplet was first given by Our Lord to St. Faustina Kowalska (1905-1938). By praying this chaplet, we ask God to have mercy on us and on all sinners throughout the world, including those who do not know how to pray for themselves. We unite ourselves to Jesus' own self-offering on the Cross and in the Holy Sacrifice of the Mass in order to atone for (that is, make up for; say we are sorry for) our sins and the sins of all people throughout the world.

The entire chaplet takes about eight minutes to pray. Ideally, it would be prayed at the Hour of Divine Mercy, 3:00 p.m., the hour Christ died on the Cross. It is a powerful prayer to say for those who are sick or dying. It is also a perfect prayer to say in the car or anytime you may be waiting or find yourself (or a loved one) in need of mercy.

Misericordia

HOW TO PRAY THE DIVINE MERCY CHAPLET

1. Choose a person to be the Leader. The Leader will pray aloud the words prefaced with a "℣." (for "Versicle," the leading passage). The rest of the family will respond by praying the words prefaced with an "℟." (for "Response," the complementary passage).

2. Proceed as follows:

   ℣. Are there any intentions you have for this Divine Mercy Chaplet?

   ℟. [Those who have intentions can mention them aloud at this time. When there are no more intentions to mention, the Leader proceeds.]

The Sign of the Cross

℣. In the name of the Father, and of the Son, and of the Holy Spirit.

℟. Amen.

[Optional Opening Prayer is on page 127.]

The Our Father

℣. Our Father, who art in heaven, hallowed be Thy name. Thy kingdom come. Thy will be done, on earth as it is in heaven.

℟. Give us this day our daily bread, and forgive us our trespasses, as we forgive those who trespass against us. And lead us not into temptation, but deliver us from evil. Amen.

The Hail Mary

℣. Hail Mary, full of grace, the Lord is with thee. Blessed art thou among women, and blessed is the fruit of thy womb, Jesus.

℟. Holy Mary, Mother of God, pray for us sinners now and at the hour of our death. Amen.

The Apostles' Creed

℣. I believe in God, the Father Almighty, Creator of heaven and earth; and in Jesus Christ, His only Son Our Lord, who was conceived by the Holy Spirit, born of the Virgin Mary, suffered under Pontius Pilate, was crucified, died, and was buried. He descended into hell; the third day He rose again from the dead; He ascended into heaven, and is seated at the right hand of God, the Father Almighty; from thence He shall come to judge the living and the dead.

℟. I believe in the Holy Spirit, the holy Catholic Church, the communion of saints, the forgiveness of sins, the resurrection of the body, and life everlasting. Amen.

THE DECADES

[Use this structure for each of the five (5) decades.]

(On the large/separated bead)

℣. Eternal Father, I offer You the Body and Blood, Soul and Divinity of Your dearly beloved Son, Our Lord Jesus Christ,

℟. in atonement for our sins and those of the whole world.

(On each of the 10 smaller/grouped beads)

℣. For the sake of His sorrowful Passion,

℟. have mercy on us and on the whole world.

After the five decades are completed:

Concluding Doxology

℣. Holy God,

℟. Holy Mighty One, Holy Immortal One, have mercy on us and on the whole world.

℣. Holy God,

℟. Holy Mighty One, Holy Immortal One, have mercy on us and on the whole world.

℣. Holy God,

℟. Holy Mighty One, Holy Immortal One, have mercy on us and on the whole world.

[Optional Concluding Prayer is below.]

℣. Eternal God, in whom mercy is endless and the treasury of compassion inexhaustible, look kindly upon us and increase Your mercy in us, that in difficult moments we might not despair nor become despondent, but with great confidence submit ourselves to Your holy will, which is Love and Mercy itself.

℟. Amen.

Concluding Sign of the Cross

℣. In the name of the Father, and of the Son, and of the Holy Spirit.

℟. Amen.

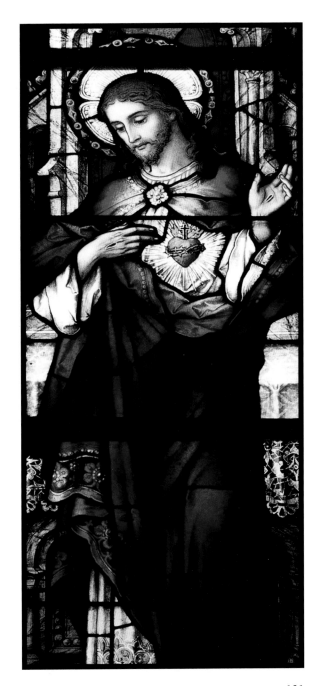

[T]HE GREATEST
ATTRIBUTE
OF GOD
IS
LOVE AND MERCY.

SAINT FAUSTINA

EUCHARISTIC ADORATION AS A FAMILY

THE DIVINE PRAISES

Blessed be God.
Blessed be His holy name.
Blessed be Jesus Christ, true God and true man.
Blessed be the name of Jesus.
Blessed be His Most Sacred Heart.
Blessed be His Most Precious Blood.
Blessed be Jesus
in the Most Holy Sacrament of the Altar.
Blessed be the Holy Spirit, the Paraclete.
Blessed be the great Mother of God,
Mary most holy.
Blessed be her holy and Immaculate Conception.
Blessed be her glorious Assumption.
Blessed be the name of Mary,
Virgin and Mother.
Blessed be Saint Joseph, her most chaste spouse.
Blessed be God in His angels and in His Saints.

Jesus Christ is with us. In the Most Blessed Sacrament of the Altar, the Eucharist, the same Jesus who walked this earth 2,000 years ago is present—Body, Blood, Soul, and Divinity. He dwells among us through the Eucharist. He is present to us and in our lives through the Eucharist, inviting us anew to stay with Him and pray. Eucharistic Adoration is worshiping, praising, thanking, interceding, asking forgiveness, and adoring Our Lord present in the Blessed Sacrament.

Historically, Eucharistic Adoration began because the Blessed Sacrament was reserved in a special place in the church so that it might be brought to the sick when needed. The faithful, recognizing the Real Presence of Our Lord, began the practice of praying in the presence of the Blessed Sacrament. Eucharistic Adoration both extends our thanksgiving from the time we last received Holy Communion and prepares us for our next Mass, where we will receive Our Lord in Holy Communion again.

On the night before He was to suffer and die, Jesus asked His disciples, "Stay awake and pray with me" (cf. Mt 26:41); after the Resurrection, His disciples would in turn ask Jesus, "Stay with us, [Lord]" (Lk 24:29).

Your whole family or one spouse and the older children can take turns spending one hour or a half-hour in Eucharistic Adoration once a week or once a month. It is a beautiful practice that will bring graces to your whole family. Parishes have different arrangements for Eucharistic Adoration. Once you have determined the time and the place your family can go for Eucharistic Adoration, briefly prepare for it by bringing with you the rosaries, books, or the personal prayer journals you will need for Adoration. If you have young children, bring holy cards, a children's Bible, or another collection of sacred images that the children can look at during Adoration. Some parishes have libraries and/or Adoration chapels with small libraries of helpful resources. It is best to decide how you will spend your Adoration time before you enter the Eucharistic Adoration chapel since most Eucharistic Adoration chapels are silent (that is, everyone prays quietly rather than praying or speaking aloud).

The following are ways you and your children may pray during Eucharistic Adoration:

1. Personal Prayer (with optional journaling). Use the time simply to speak to the Lord as you would to a close friend, telling Him what is in your heart and on your mind— things you are worried about; people you promised to pray for or would like to pray for; giving thanks; going over the week with Him, etc. Then, spend time listening to Him, just as you stop to listen to what your friend has to say in response to you. If you would like, you could do this in a journal form, writing a letter to God. A simple and beautiful traditional formula for prayer (and journaling) can be remembered with the acronym "ACTS."

A = Adoration. Adore the Lord. Worship Him as God. Praise Him. Glorify Him. Love Him. Enjoy being in His presence.

C = Contrition. Apologize to the Lord for any sins you may have committed. You may also apologize for any faults or weaknesses that you have given in to. Ask Him for His help in your resolution to change, to avoid these sins, faults, and weaknesses. Then, allow Him to embrace you spiritually. He loves you. There is no sin you could ever commit that would cause Him to stop loving you. Accept His forgiveness and love.

T = Thanksgiving. Thank the Lord for His forgiveness, for His presence in your life. Thank Him for as many specific blessings as you can think of.

S = Seeking or Supplication. Ask the Lord for whatever you need. Ask Him for the blessings and graces that you and others need.

2. Pray the Rosary, meditating on the life of Jesus who is before you in the Blessed Sacrament.

3. Read the Scriptures and meditate on them. You can read the Gospel for the day or any part of the Gospel. Place yourself in the Gospel scene, ask questions about the scene

and people in it, and be attentive to what the Lord may be showing you through that Gospel scene.

4. Decades of Gratitude. Take a rosary and, using one set of ten beads, kneel before the Blessed Sacrament and thank the Lord for ten specific blessings (persons, events, occurrences, gifts, conversations, etc.) of the past week. On each bead, simply say, "Thank you, Lord, for ____." Or, take a rosary and, using the 50 beads, thank God for the 50 greatest blessings of your life, naming each one specifically, one per bead.

5. Spiritual Reading. Read a book about the life of one of the saints. The saints are our brothers and sisters, members of our Catholic Family Tree! Their examples can help us, inspire us, and comfort us. And, still more, the saints themselves can intercede for us and help us from heaven. They are magnificent friends to have.

Close your Eucharistic Adoration time with the Divine Praises (page 133).

You will find that Eucharistic Adoration can bring you clarity and peace of mind. Through it, your whole family can grow closer to Our Lord and love Him more in the Blessed Sacrament.

PHASE FIVE

MAKING YOUR LIFE
A PRAYER

LIVING THE VIRTUES

ASPIRATIONS

MORE WAYS TO PRAY

LIVING THE VIRTUES

Come Holy Spirit,
fill the hearts of Your faithful
and enkindle in them the fire of Your love.
℣. Send forth Your Spirit,
and they shall be created.
℟. And You shall renew
the face of the earth.

Let us pray:

O God,
who by the light of the Holy Spirit
did instruct the hearts of the faithful,
grant us through the same Spirit
a love and relish for
what is right and just
and a constant enjoyment of His consolation,
through Christ Our Lord.
Amen.

Love is patient, love is kind. It is not jealous, [love] is not pompous, it is not inflated, it is not rude, it does not seek its own interests, it is not quick-tempered, it does not brood over injury, it does not rejoice over wrongdoing but rejoices with the truth. It bears all things, believes all things, hopes all things, endures all things. Love never fails. . . . So faith, hope, love remain, these three; but the greatest of these is love (1 Cor 13:4-8,13).

What St. Paul gives us here is a brief introduction to the virtues (holy habits of loving well) and the vices (bad habits of selfishness). As a family, you can read and discuss this passage together, asking how the virtues of patience and kindness can be lived concretely in your family (e.g., waiting patiently in the car for others; or, if you are the person others are waiting for, doing your best to get to the car quickly). You can also discuss the vices: being jealous, pompous, inflated, rude, self-seeking, etc. When you discuss the virtues and vices, as well as the definitions and examples of each, you will begin to be more aware of how to live the virtues and avoid the vices.

Essential to the Christian life are love of God and love of neighbor. These are the two greatest commandments (cf. Mk 12:28-31). Our family members are our closest neighbors. But, we live so closely with them that we can take for granted the great gift that each one truly is. What are the signs that we really do love each other? St. Paul tells us:

As Christians, we should all be working to avoid mortal sins and everyday faults (or venial sins). It is through the hard work of fighting against our sinful tendencies that we grow in holiness. Gossip and envy damage us spiritually, as do being bossy, nagging others, failing to fulfill responsibilities or contribute to the family, throwing temper tantrums, complaining, overeating, competing with others in a negative way, bullying, and giving in to jealousy. When we are attentive to the Lord and His Word, He will help us to see what we need to work on. His love and His grace are greater than all our sins and weaknesses.

As we work with the Lord to root out the bad, we should also work with Him to plant the good. So, we should begin to practice more acts of kindness and courtesy, being thoughtful of others (e.g., not always taking the best for ourselves, leaving the biggest piece of pizza or dessert for someone else), asking others what they would like instead of wanting things always done our way, anticipating others' needs, and being sensitive to others' likes and dislikes. If you strive to be attentive, gentle, kind, and generous to one another, you will find that you are loving one another.

A simple format for Living the Virtues is this:

1. After breakfast on the first Saturday or Sunday of the month, as a family discuss one of the Scripture passages given in this section.

2. Choose a virtue you would like to work on together.

3. Discuss concrete examples of how you can live that virtue.

4. Discuss the vice that is the opposite of that virtue, including examples of the vice [e.g., virtue = patience; vice = impatience, annoyance, complaining].

5. Post the "Virtue of the Month" on your family prayer board (or the refrigerator).

6. Add the little aspiration "Lord, help us to grow in the virtue of ___" after Grace at Meals.

7. Praise the family members whom you see practicing the virtue. Encourage one another all month.

By consciously striving to live the virtues and drive out the vices, you will find that your family begins to grow more holy! Since you will work on a different virtue each month, this means that by the end of a year, you will all have grown in 12 different virtues. This means you will have grown in loving God and one another.

If you would like another resource to help with your family discussion of the virtues, please see the sections in the *Catechism of the Catholic Church* on the virtues, the Beatitudes, and the Gifts of the Holy Spirit.

SCRIPTURE PASSAGES FOR FAMILY VIRTUE DISCUSSIONS

Let love be sincere; hate what is evil, hold on to what is good; love one another with mutual affection; anticipate one another in showing honor. Do not grow slack in zeal, be fervent in spirit, serve the Lord. Rejoice in hope, endure in affliction, persevere in prayer. Contribute to the needs of the holy ones; exercise hospitality. Bless those who persecute [you]; bless and do not curse them. Rejoice with those who rejoice, weep with those who weep. Have the same regard for one another; do not be haughty but associate with the lowly; do not be wise in your own estimation. Do not repay anyone evil for evil; be concerned for what is noble in the sight of all. If possible, on your part, live at peace with all. Beloved, do not look for revenge but leave room for the wrath; for it is written, "Vengeance is mine, I will repay, says the Lord." Rather, "if your enemy is hungry, feed him; if he is thirsty, give him something to drink . . ." Do not be conquered by evil but conquer evil with good (Rom 12:9-21).

Owe nothing to anyone, except to love one another; for the one who loves another has fulfilled the law. The commandments, "You shall not commit adultery; you shall not kill; you shall not steal; you shall not covet," and whatever other commandment there may be, are summed up in this saying, [namely] "You shall love your neighbor as yourself." Love does no evil to the neighbor; hence, love is the fulfillment of the law. And do this because you know the time; it is the hour now for you to awake from sleep. For our salvation is nearer now than when we first believed; the night is advanced, the day

S · DOMINIC

is at hand. Let us then throw off the works of darkness [and] put on the armor of light; let us conduct ourselves properly as in the day, not in . . . drunkenness, not in promiscuity and licentiousness, not in rivalry and jealousy. But put on the Lord Jesus Christ, and make no provision for the desires of the flesh (Rom 13:8-14).

Live by the Spirit and you will certainly not gratify the desire of the flesh. For the flesh has desires against the Spirit, and the Spirit against the flesh; these are opposed to each other, so that you may not do what you want. But if you are guided by the Spirit, you are not under the law. Now the works of the flesh are obvious: immorality, impurity, licentiousness, idolatry, sorcery, hatreds, rivalry, jealousy, outbursts of fury, acts of selfishness, dissensions, factions, occasions of envy, drinking bouts . . . and the like. I warn you, as I warned you before, that those who do such things will not inherit the kingdom of God. In contrast, the fruit of the Spirit is love, joy, peace, patience, kindness, generosity, faithfulness, gentleness, self-control. Against such there is no law. Now those who belong to Christ [Jesus] have crucified their flesh with its passions and desires. If we live in the Spirit, let us also follow the Spirit. Let us not be conceited, provoking one another, envious of one another (Gal 5:16-26).

Therefore, putting away falsehood, speak the truth, each one to his neighbor, for we are members one of another. Be angry but do not sin; do not let the sun set on your anger, and do not leave room for the devil. The thief must no longer steal, but rather labor, doing honest work with his [own] hands, so that he may have something to share with one in need. No foul language should come out of your mouths, but only such as is good for needed edification, that it may impart grace to those who hear. And do not grieve the holy Spirit of God, with which you were sealed for the day of redemption. All bitterness, fury, anger, shouting, and reviling must be removed from you, along with all malice. [And] be kind to one another, compassionate, forgiving one another as God has forgiven you in Christ (Eph 4:25-32).

So be imitators of God, as beloved children, and live in love, as Christ loved us and handed Himself over for us as a sacrificial offering to God for a fragrant aroma. Immorality or any impurity or greed must not even be mentioned among you, as is fitting among holy ones, no obscenity or silly or suggestive talk, which is out of place, but instead, thanksgiving. Be sure of this, that no immoral or impure or greedy person, that is, an idolater, has any inheritance in the kingdom of Christ and of God. Let no one

deceive you with empty arguments, for because of these things the wrath of God is coming upon the disobedient. So do not be associated with them. For you were once darkness, but now you are light in the Lord. Live as children of light, for light produces every kind of goodness and righteousness and truth. Try to learn what is pleasing to the Lord (Eph 5:1-10).

Rejoice always. Pray without ceasing. In all circumstances give thanks, for this is the will of God for you in Christ Jesus (1 Thes 5:16-18).

This is how all will know that you are my disciples, if you have love for one another (Jn 13:35).

PRAY NOT ONLY
WITH YOUR LIPS
BUT WITH
YOUR LIVES.

SAINT AUGUSTINE

ASPIRATIONS

Pray without ceasing.

1 Thessalonians 5:17

The fervent prayer
of a righteous person
is very powerful.

James 5:16

[T]he Spirit too
comes to the aid of our weakness;
for we do not know
how to pray as we ought,
but the Spirit [Himself] intercedes
with inexpressible groanings.

Romans 8:26

❧ My God, I love Thee.

❧ Jesus, I love You.

❧ My Jesus, mercy.

❧ Come, Lord Jesus, I need You.

❧ Praised be Jesus Christ, now and forever.

❧ Jesus, meek and humble of Heart, make my heart like unto Thine.

❧ Sacred Heart of Jesus, Thy kingdom come!

❧ Sacred Heart of Jesus, protect our family!

❧ Sacred Heart of Jesus, have mercy on us.

❧ Jesus is Lord!

❧ Thank You, Jesus!

❧ We adore You, O Christ, and we praise You, because by Your holy Cross You have redeemed the world.

❧ Lord, teach me to do Your will.

❧ By myself I can do nothing, but with You, Lord, I can do all things.

❧ Blessed be God!

❧ Jesus, Mary, I love you. Save souls!

❧ Come, Holy Mary, please help me.

❧ Immaculate Heart of Mary, pray for us.

❧ Mary, conceived without sin, pray for us who have recourse to you.

❧ I am all yours, my Queen and my Mother, and all that I have is yours.[1]

❧ Virgin Mary, Mother of Jesus, help us to become saints.[2]

---

[1] From the Legion of Mary.

[2] This list of traditional and suggested aspirations was compiled by the Dominican Sisters of St. Cecilia.

Aspirations are a wonderful way to quickly turn our minds and hearts toward God throughout the day or in times of need. An aspiration (literally, "a breath"; "a sigh") is a very short prayer, such as, "Jesus, I love You!" or "Jesus, I trust in You." They can be said aloud or quietly within. In the tradition of the Church, it has been said that aspirations are like arrows that we shoot up to heaven so quickly that they pierce the clouds and reach the throne of God, bringing us immediately into God's presence. They take very little time to pray and yet can be very effective. Aspirations help us to converse with God throughout the day and to remember Him, our ever-present Friend and Companion. Just as we grow in friendship with others by regular and frequent conversation and sharing of daily life, so too do we grow in our friendship with God by regular conversation and sharing with Him our daily activities, joys, and concerns. Aspirations help us to see with the eyes of faith.

A charming story[3] illustrates the power of praying aspirations:

---

[3] We were unable to determine the precise origin of this story, also told by Venerable Fulton J. Sheen.

In a village in France, many years ago, there were two young boys who were the best of friends. Both boys were Catholic, and their mothers had them walk to the neighborhood church for Confession every Saturday morning. Sometimes, they would race one another to the church. At other times, they would walk slowly along, not really wanting to go to Confession. One particular Saturday morning, the rambunctious boys were bouncing along on their way to the church for Confession, planning together all the things they would do after they finished their Confessions and said their penances. Then, it occurred to one of them to initiate a game: "Let's have a contest: whoever gets out of Confession and finishes his penance first, WINS!" The other boy eagerly replied, "Agreed."

Two priests happened to be hearing Confessions that morning, so that each of the boys was able to go into Confession almost immediately. Inside the confessional, when the first boy had finished his Confession, the priest said to him, "For your penance, would you please kneel before the Crucifix and say three times: 'Jesus, You have done everything for me, and I have done nothing for You'?" Thrilled at receiving such a short and easy penance, the boy, replied "Yes, Father!" and began rejoicing, thinking, "I'm going to win the contest! I know

I will finish first!" He quickly went to kneel in front of the crucifix and said, "Jesus, You have done everything for me, and I have done nothing for You." He said it a second time— "Jesus, You have done everything for me, and I have done nothing for You"—and just then it struck deep into his heart precisely what he was saying, and the little boy didn't get up from his knees but remained there, lost in prayer, adoration, and thanksgiving. He later became a cardinal of the Catholic Church.

This beautiful aspiration, "Jesus, You have done everything for me, and I have done nothing for You," changed his life. The same can happen for each of us. An aspiration can be a grace that changes our life. There are many common aspirations (as found on page 151), but there is no fixed form that would limit the number or type of aspirations that you could pray. You can create your own aspirations to suit your own particular needs or struggles, such as, "Jesus, help me to trust You more and to worry less."

You can have young children decorate aspirations and put them at eye-level in different places around the house (refrigerator, bathroom mirrors, hallway, laundry room, Mom and Dad's room, etc.) to help remind everyone to pray them.

MORE WAYS TO PRAY

Praise the LORD, all you nations!
Extol him, all you peoples!

His mercy for us is strong;
the faithfulness of the LORD is forever.

PSALM 117

Congratulations! May the Lord be praised for having brought you and your family this far in your journey toward Him. As you continue to grow in prayer as a family and individually, you may consider incorporating some of the following into your family life.

- Attend the Holy Sacrifice of the Mass on one or more weekdays.

- Pray the Act of Contrition (at the end of each day, or at the end of Family Bedtime Prayers).

- Pray the Angelus (This traditional prayer—prayed three times a day—recalls the fact that Christ became man to redeem us.).

- Celebrate the liturgical feasts and seasons as a family (Prepare an Advent wreath; pray the Stations of the Cross together on the Fridays in Lent, etc.). There are resources available with ideas for celebrating the Liturgical Year in the home.

- Set Sunday aside as a special time for family, prayer, and service (such as visiting relatives and/or the sick).

- Have family Scripture study and discussion (Wednesday nights or another week night).

- Offer a "Media Fast" (sacrifice the use of technology for days, weeks, Advent, Lent, or certain times of the day) and do something as a family instead (Scripture discussion, book discussion, or a family service activity).

- Visit the cemetery to pray for the dead (especially in the first week of November, the anniversary of a loved one's death, and Memorial Day).

- Pray the Divine Office (The Liturgy of the Hours).

- Pray novenas for special occasions or intentions.

- Increase parish involvement (Join or start prayer or study groups, service activities, special days for families, married couple retreats, etc.).

- Have a Mass offered for family members on their birthdays and/or name days.

- Consider giving religious items or spiritual bouquets (i.e., offerings of a certain number and kind of prayers for the recipients and their intentions) as gifts.

- Celebrate your patron saints' feast days.

- Wear the Brown Scapular.

- Celebrate anniversaries of receiving the sacraments (Baptism, First Confession, First Holy Communion, Confirmation, Matrimony, etc.).

- Pray the Acts of Faith, Hope, and Charity.

Remember that everything in life has a balance, and your family always comes first. Loving and serving your spouse and your children is one of the primary ways you love and serve Our Lord. Together, you and your spouse can help keep one another and your children balanced, holy, healthy, and happy. May your friendship with the Lord continue to deepen as you "pray always" (cf. 1 Thes 5:17) and live in union with Him throughout each day. He longs to have a personal relationship with each one of you and to be more and more a part of your lives. Let Him enter, the King of Glory!

APPENDIX

THE STAINED GLASS TRADITION

BY DR. DENIS MCNAMARA

In the theology of St. Thomas Aquinas, Beauty is called the attractive power of the Truth, that "something extra" which makes the Truth not only knowable, but delightful. To experience a beautiful stained glass window is to encounter this attractive power. Even before we understand the content of a window, we are caught up in light and color. In delight the mind is led to investigate the theological ideas presented in the window, and soon we ponder the things of God in easy cooperation, moving out of ourselves and toward something good. This movement of the will toward the Good is a traditional definition of love. Stained glass windows, then, are not simply pretty pictures, but spiritual aids in the process of coming to know God who is radiant, generous Love itself.

The earliest examples of man-made glass date to Egypt in about 2750 BC, with beads and decorative containers of different types. In the ancient Roman Empire, vessels were composed of twisted, carved, and molded glass. Small glass pieces were even sometimes assembled into windows. But these were not the dramatic stained glass windows we think of today. The gem-like radiance of figural stained glass can rightly be called a Christian art, since it was developed entirely within the Christian context. The earliest known ecclesiastical stained glass windows date from the ninth century, marking the beginning of a great flowering of stained glass into the thirteenth and fourteenth centuries. Despite many ups and downs in popularity and style, the art of stained glass making has continued to this day.

No matter what the content of any particular stained glass window, a few theological points help them come alive. Salvation history teaches that in the beginning, humanity and creation were in right relationship with God, as Adam and Eve walked in harmony with the Father in the Garden of Eden. The disobedience of our first parents caused a rupture known as the Fall, affecting man's intellect, will, and relationships with God, each other and creation. The Bible teaches clearly of God's loving mission of salvation, indicated by prophets, kings, priests and the rules of right worship, all culminating in Christ. Old Testament prophets speak frequently of the desert becoming a garden again, while the Temple of Solomon was decorated with garden imagery overlaid with gold. Mary Magdalene even confuses the risen Christ with the gardener, a rich biblical idea of Jesus as the New Adam who restores man to

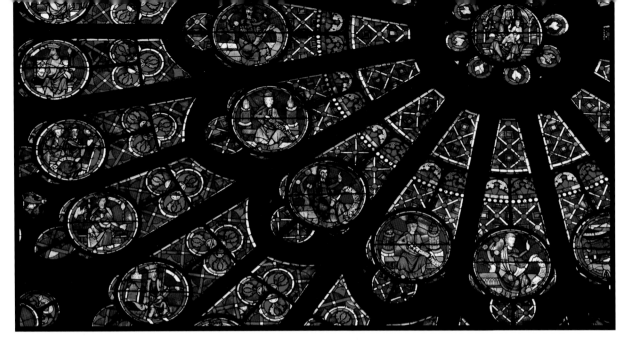

paradise. Moreover, scripture frequently uses the idea of gems to represent three things: right relationship with God, glorified humanity and restored creation. This relationship between gem and garden finds completion in the Book of Revelation, where the New Earth meets the New Heaven: a heavenly garden is surrounded with walls made of gems and is filled with angels and saints praising God.

So when you look at stained glass windows, see the New Heaven and the New Earth. Imagine a wall of gem-like radiance with the blue of sapphires and the red of rubies which form images of God, saints, angels and the New Earth, all of which is suffused by light. Smaller windows frequently display borders with vines, leaves, and flowers intertwined with people and even animals. On the larger scale, rose windows form great spoke-like wheels with Christ at the center, surrounded by the orderly array of heavenly beings, nature and even sacred history taken up into eternity. So delighting in the light of a stained glass window is delighting in one of the best images we can have on earth of our own heavenly future. The truth—the reality of our hoped-for happiness in the light of God's face—is presented to our minds and hearts, and the result is delight and love.

Denis R. McNamara, Ph.D., is an architectural historian specializing in sacred art and architecture. He is the Associate Director of the Liturgical Institute at Chicago's Mundelein Seminary, the University of Saint Mary of the Lake.

IMAGE CREDITS

The author and publisher gratefully acknowledge the permission granted to reproduce the copyrighted material in this book.

Every effort has been made to trace copyright holders and to obtain their permission for the use of copyrighted material. The author and publisher apologize for any errors or omissions in the list below and would be grateful to be notified of any corrections that should be incorporated in future reprints or editions of this book.

All photographs © 2015 by Father Lawrence Lew, O.P., unless otherwise noted.

FRONT COVER IMAGE: The Holy Family with St. Anne, Hardman of Birmingham, UK, 1890; Downside Abbey Church, Bath, UK. Courtesy of Downside Abbey Trustees.

3 The Holy Family with St. Anne, Hardman of Birmingham, UK, 1890; Downside Abbey Church, Bath, UK. Courtesy of Downside Abbey Trustees.

5 The Christ Child speaking to His Mother, Sir Ninian Comper, c. 1937; Pusey House Chapel, Oxford, UK. Courtesy of the Principal and Chapter of Pusey House, Oxford, UK.

6 An angel swinging a thurible (detail), Charles Eamer Kempe, c. 1900; St. Hilda's Priory Chapel, Sneaton, North Yorkshire, UK.

7 An angel swinging a thurible (detail), Charles Eamer Kempe, c. 1900; St. John the Evangelist Church, Oxford, UK.

8 Christ entering Jerusalem, James Ballantine & Son of Edinburgh, UK, 1875; St. Giles' Cathedral, Edinburgh, UK.

10 To the Glory of God: Detail from the Macnutt Memorial Window, A.E. Buss, 1956, Leicester Cathedral, St. Dunstan's Chapel, Leicester, UK. Image used by permission of the Dean and Chapter of Leicester Cathedral.

12 St. Mary Magdalene meets the risen Christ, Burlison & Grylls, c. 1922; St. Mary in the Lace Market, Nottingham, UK. Courtesy of the Nottingham Churches.

14 St. Dominic preaching the Rosary (detail), c. 1883; St. Dominic's Priory Church, London, UK. Courtesy of St. Dominic's Priory Church, London, UK.

17 The Good Shepherd (detail), c. 1860s; St. Mary the Virgin, Buckland, Oxfordshire, UK.

18 The Annunciation, Clayton & Bell, UK, c. 1859-60, by permission of the Rector, Fellows, and Scholars of Exeter College in the University of Oxford.

20-21 Christ carries His Cross, Werkstatt Henning und Andres, Germany, 1908; Market

Church of Sts. George & James, Hannover, Germany. Courtesy of the Market Church of Sts. George & James, Hannover, Germany.

23 The Crucifixion scene, James Ballantine & Son of Edinburgh, UK, c. 1877; St. Giles' Cathedral, Edinburgh, UK.

24 Jesse window (detail), Augustus Welby Pugin (fabricated by William Wailes), 1844; The Cathedral Church of St. Mary, Newcastle-up-on-Tyne, UK.

25 Charity personified (detail), Edward Burne-Jones, c. 1895-99; Harris Manchester College Chapel, Oxford, UK.

27 Eli and the young Samuel (detail), Edward Burne-Jones, c. 1872-3; Christ Church Cathedral, Oxford, UK.

28 The Annunciation (detail) c. 1884; St. Cuthbert's College, Ushaw, Ushaw Moor, Durham, UK.

29 The Virgin and Child (detail), c. 1884; St. Cuthbert's College, Ushaw, Ushaw Moor, Durham, UK.

30 The Shield of the Assumption (detail), 1953; The Roman Catholic National Shrine of Our Lady, Walsingham, England (The Slipper Chapel). Stained glass window © by Roman Catholic National Shrine of Our Lady, Walsingham, England. Courtesy of The Roman Catholic National Shrine of Our Lady, Walsingham, England.

31 The Virgin with the Christ Child speaking to her (detail), Sir Ninian Comper, 1945; St. Alban the Martyr Church, Holborn, London, UK. Courtesy of the Parochial Church Council of St. Alban's, Holborn.

32 Christ interceding for us before the Father (detail), Augustus C. Pugin, c. 1840; St. Chad's Cathedral, Birmingham, UK.

33 The Holy Spirit (detail), Edward W. Heimer & Co., Clifton, NJ, c. 1965; St. Dominic's Church, Washington, D.C. Courtesy of St. Dominic's Church, Washington, D.C.

35 Shield of the Trinity held by two angels, c. 1900; St. Andrew's Church, Newcastle-up-on-Tyne, UK.

36 Mary and Joseph receive lodging (detail), c. 1883; St. Dominic's Priory Church, London, UK. Courtesy of St. Dominic's Priory Church, London, UK.

39 Jesus reveals His Sacred Heart to St. Margaret Mary (detail), 1880s; St. Patrick Church, Columbus, OH.

41 The Christ Child with the Blessed Virgin Mary (detail), c. 1827; St. Cuthbert's Church, Durham, UK.

42 Christ the King (detail), Charles Eamer Kempe, c. 1870s-1880s; St Michael's Church, Cumnor, Oxford, UK.

43 St. Thomas More praying to the Our Lady (detail), 1911; Harvington Hall, Harvington,

Kidderminster, Worcestershire, UK. Courtesy of Harvington Hall.

44 Angels kneeling in adoration (detail), Clayton & Bell, UK, c. 1893; St. Mary's Episcopal Cathedral, Glasgow, UK.

45 The Ordination of seven deacons, Clayton & Bell, UK, c. 1865, by permission of the Rector, Fellows, and Scholars of Exeter College in the University of Oxford.

46-47 Jesus shares the Last Supper with His apostles (and detail), James Ballantine & Son of Edinburgh, UK, c. 1869; St. Giles' Cathedral, Edinburgh, UK.

48 The pelican feeds its young, Franz Mayer of Munich, Germany, 2006-2008; St. Cecilia Motherhouse sacristy, Nashville, TN. Photograph © 2015 by St. Cecilia Congregation, LBP Communications. All rights reserved.

50 The fall of manna, Clayton & Bell, UK, 1859-1860, by permission of the Rector, Fellows, and Scholars of Exeter College in the University of Oxford.

51 Supper at Emmaus (detail), Clayton & Bell, UK, c. 1868; St. Mary the Virgin, Freeland, Oxfordshire, UK.

52 A mother and two children (detail), c. 1800; Glasgow Cathedral, Glasgow, UK. Courtesy of Glasgow Cathedral.

53 The Child Jesus is found in the Temple (detail), Franz Mayer of Munich, Germany, 1910-1913; Cathedral Basilica of the Assumption, Covington, KY. Courtesy of the Cathedral Basilica of the Assumption, Covington, KY. Photograph © 2015 by St. Cecilia Congregation, LBP Communications. All rights reserved.

54-55 Fathers and mothers bringing their children to the Lord (detail), George Gilbert Scott, c. 1864-74; Bath Abbey, Bath, Somerset, UK.

56 St. John the Evangelist (detail), Geoffrey Webb, c. 1924; Ampleforth Abbey, Ampleforth, UK. Courtesy of Ampleforth Abbey.

57 The Presentation of Christ at the Temple, Hardman of Birmingham, UK, 1890; Downside Abbey Church, Bath, UK. Courtesy of Downside Abbey Trustees.

58 Christ and His Apostles (detail), Franz Mayer of Munich, Germany, 1910-1913; Cathedral Basilica of the Assumption, Covington, KY. Courtesy of the Cathedral Basilica of the Assumption, Covington, KY. Photograph © 2015 by St. Cecilia Congregation, LBP Communications. All rights reserved.

59 A woman and children looking at Our Lord (detail), Franz Mayer of Munich, Germany, 1910-1913; Cathedral Basilica of the Assumption, Covington, KY. Courtesy of the Cathedral Basilica of the Assumption, Covington, KY. Photograph © 2015 by St. Cecilia Congregation, LBP Communications. All rights reserved.

60 Jesus working with St. Joseph (detail), Sir Ninian Comper, c. 1913; St. Mary and St. John's Church, Cowley, Oxford, UK. Courtesy of St. Mary and St. John's Church, Cowley, Oxford, UK.

61 St. Anne teaching Mary (detail), Sir Ninian Comper, c. 1913; St. Mary and St. John's Church, Cowley, Oxford, UK. Courtesy of St. Mary and St. John's Church, Cowley, Oxford, UK.

62 The birth of St. John the Baptist (detail), c. 1880; St. John the Baptist Church, Glastonbury, Somerset, UK. Stained glass window © by St. John the Baptist Church, Glastonbury. Courtesy of the Parochial Church Council of St. John the Baptist Church, Glastonbury.

63 The Good Shepherd (detail), Jean-Baptiste Capronnier, c. 1860; Holy Trinity Church, Skipton, North Yorkshire, UK.

64 Mary, the flower of Sts. Joachim and Anne (detail), c. 1890; St. James Roman Catholic Church, Spanish Place, London, UK. Courtesy of St. James Roman Catholic Church, Spanish Place, London, UK.

65 Joachim and Anne meet at the city gates (detail), 1517-1520; Church of St. Gervase and St. Protase, Paris, France.

67 The marriage of the Virgin Mary to St. Joseph (detail), Clayton & Bell, UK, c. 1869; St. Mary the Virgin, Freeland, Oxfordshire, UK.

68 A family praying the Rosary together (detail), c. 1955-1958; Roman Catholic Church of Our Lady of the Victories, Kensington, London, UK. Courtesy of Roman Catholic Church of Our Lady of the Victories, Kensington, London, UK.

69 The Blessed Mother and the Rosary (detail), c. 1955-1958; Roman Catholic Church of Our Lady of the Victories, Kensington, London, UK. Courtesy of Roman Catholic Church of Our Lady of the Victories, Kensington, London, UK.

70 St. Dominic and the Rosary (detail), c. 1955-1958; Roman Catholic Church of Our Lady of the Victories, Kensington, London, UK. Courtesy of Roman Catholic Church of Our Lady of the Victories, Kensington, London, UK.

73 A rosary with the Annunciation scene inside (detail), Charles Eamer Kempe, c. 1905; Sidney Sussex College Chapel, Cambridge, UK.

74-75 Our Blessed Mother gives the Rosary to St. Dominic (detail), c. 1883; St. Dominic's Priory Church, London, UK. Courtesy of St. Dominic's Priory Church, London, UK.

77 Our Lady of Lourdes, c. 1883; St. Dominic's Priory Church, London, UK. Courtesy of St. Dominic's Priory Church, London, UK.

78 Jesus calms the storm at sea (detail), Franz Mayer of Munich, Germany, 1910-1913; Cathedral Basilica of the Assumption, Covington,

KY. Courtesy of the Cathedral Basilica of the Assumption, Covington, KY. Photograph © 2015 by St. Cecilia Congregation, LBP Communications. All rights reserved.

80 Candlemas angels (detail), Harry Clarke, c. 1889; Chapel of the Sisters of Notre Dame de Namur, Oxford, UK.

81 The Annunciation (detail), Harry Clarke, c. 1889; Chapel of the Sisters of Notre Dame de Namur, Oxford, UK.

82 St. Raphael the Archangel and Tobias (detail), c. 1825; St. Mary's at Harvington, Kidderminster, Worcestershire, UK.

83 The Annunciation (detail), James Powell, c. 1885; Trinity College, Oxford , UK.

84 The face of St. Michael the Archangel (detail), James Powell & Sons of Whitehall, UK, 1913; St. Michael at the Northgate, Oxford, UK. Courtesy of St. Michael at the Northgate, Oxford, UK.

85 St. Michael slaying the dragon, Sir Ninian Comper, 1945; St. Alban the Martyr Church, Holborn, London, UK. Courtesy of the Parochial Church Council of St. Alban's, Holborn.

87 The three archangels with a Dominican praying the Rosary, Augustus C. Pugin, c. 1845; St. Dominic's Priory School, Pugin Chapel, Stone, Staffordshire, UK.

88 The risen Christ gives St. George the crown of eternal life (detail), c. 1890; Holy Trinity Church, Stratford-upon-Avon, UK.

89 The Prophet Daniel (detail), c. 1879; St. Mary's Cathedral, Edinburgh, UK.

90 St. Sebastian with his soldier's armor (detail), Geoffrey Webb, c. 1924; Ampleforth Abbey, Ampleforth, UK. Courtesy of Ampleforth Abbey.

91 St. Martin of Tours sharing his cloak, Herbert Hendrie, c. 1928; Ampleforth Abbey, Ampleforth, UK. Courtesy of Ampleforth Abbey.

92-93 The sacrifice of Melchizedek (and detail), Franz Mayer of Munich, Germany, 1910-1913; Cathedral Basilica of the Assumption, Covington, KY. Courtesy of the Cathedral Basilica of the Assumption, Covington, KY. Photograph © 2015 by St. Cecilia Congregation, LBP Communications. All rights reserved.

94 The multiplication of the loaves (detail), Franz Mayer of Munich, Germany, 1910-1913; Cathedral Basilica of the Assumption, Covington, KY. Courtesy of the Cathedral Basilica of the Assumption, Covington, KY. Photograph © 2015 by St. Cecilia Congregation, LBP Communications. All rights reserved.

97 The miracle at the wedding feast of Cana (detail), Franz Mayer of Munich, Germany, 1910-1913; Cathedral Basilica of the Assumption, Covington, KY. Courtesy of the Cathedral Basilica of the Assumption, Covington, KY.

Photograph © 2015 by St. Cecilia Congregation, LBP Communications. All rights reserved.

98 The miracle of manna in the desert (detail), Franz Mayer of Munich, Germany, 1910-1913; Cathedral Basilica of the Assumption, Covington, KY. Courtesy of the Cathedral Basilica of the Assumption, Covington, KY. Photograph © 2015 by St. Cecilia Congregation, LBP Communications. All rights reserved.

100 Jesus and the little children (detail), Franz Mayer of Munich, Germany, 1910-1913; Cathedral Basilica of the Assumption, Covington, KY. Courtesy of the Cathedral Basilica of the Assumption, Covington, KY. Photograph © 2015 by St. Cecilia Congregation, LBP Communications. All rights reserved.

101 The celebration of the Passover (detail), Franz Mayer of Munich, Germany, 1910-1913; Cathedral Basilica of the Assumption, Covington, KY. Courtesy of the Cathedral Basilica of the Assumption, Covington, KY. Photograph © 2015 by St. Cecilia Congregation, LBP Communications. All rights reserved.

102 The Glorified Christ: Detail from the Macnutt Memorial Window, A.E. Buss, 1956, Leicester Cathedral, St. Dunstan's Chapel, Leicester, UK. Image used by permission of the Dean and Chapter of Leicester Cathedral.

103 The Good Samaritan (detail), c. 1860s; St. Mary the Virgin, Buckland, Oxfordshire, UK.

104 A man going to Confession and a woman saying her penance (detail), c. 1885-90; Our Lady and the English Martyrs Church, Cambridge, UK.

106 Christ and St. John, Sir Ninian Comper (detail), c. 1905-1907; All Saints Convent Chapel, Oxford, UK. Courtesy of The Society of All Saints Sisters of the Poor.

108 Jesus, the Bread of Life (detail), Alfred O. Hemming, c. 1900; St. Lawrence Church, Chicheley, UK.

109 A priest holding up the chalice (detail), designed by G. E. Street, executed by Clayton & Bell, UK, c. 1860s; St. Thomas the Martyr's Church, Oxford, UK.

110 A priest offering Mass with a family in attendance (detail), John Hardman & Company, UK, c. 1840s; St. Chad's Cathedral, Birmingham, UK.

111 Moses and the burning bush, c. 1890; St. Mary's Parish Church, Melton Mowbray, Leicestershire, UK. By kind permission of the Rector and Church Wardens of St. Mary's Parish Church, Melton Mowbray, Leicestershire, UK.

112 Moses draws water from the rock (detail), Franz Mayer of Munich, Germany, 1910-1913; Cathedral Basilica of the Assumption, Covington, KY. Courtesy of the Cathedral Basilica of the Assumption, Covington, KY. Photograph © 2015 by St. Cecilia Congregation, LBP Communications. All rights reserved.

113 The Baptism of Christ (detail), Clayton & Bell, UK, 1859-60, by permission of the Rector, Fellows, and Scholars of Exeter College in the University of Oxford.

115 Our Lady of the Rosary (detail), J.H. Mauméjean Hermanos, Madrid, Spain, 1911; Santo Cristo del Olivar, Madrid, Spain. Courtesy of the Dominicans at Santo Cristo del Olivar, Madrid, Spain.

116 The death of St. Joseph (detail), Franz Mayer of Munich, Germany, 1910-1913; Cathedral Basilica of the Assumption, Covington, KY. Courtesy of the Cathedral Basilica of the Assumption, Covington, KY. Photograph © 2015 by St. Cecilia Congregation, LBP Communications. All rights reserved.

118-119 Remembering the death of St. Thomas of Canterbury (detail), c. 1890; Holy Trinity Church, Stratford-upon-Avon, UK.

120 Our Lady makes the Sign of the Cross with St. Bernadette, c. 1899-1901; The Rosary Basilica, Lourdes, France.

121 St Gregory the Great blessing the missionaries to England, c. 1890; Downside Abbey Church, Bath, UK. Courtesy of Downside Abbey Trustees.

122 The Holy Family with St. Anne, Hardman of Birmingham, UK, 1890; Downside Abbey Church, Bath, UK. Courtesy of Downside Abbey Trustees.

123 St. Scholastica and other holy abbesses (detail), c. 1890; Downside Abbey Church, Bath, UK. Courtesy of Downside Abbey Trustees.

124-125 Performing works of mercy (detail), c. 1871; Holy Cross Church, Gilling East, North Yorkshire, UK. By permission of the Parochial Church Council of Holy Cross Church, Gilling East.

126-127 The risen Lord and St. Thomas (and detail), Franz Mayer of Munich, Germany, 1910-1913; Cathedral Basilica of the Assumption, Covington, KY. Courtesy of the Cathedral Basilica of the Assumption, Covington, KY. Photograph © 2015 by St. Cecilia Congregation, LBP Communications. All rights reserved.

128 Christ enthroned (detail), c. 1830; St Peter's and St. Paul's Church, Shiplake, Oxfordshire, UK.

129 The angel of mercy (detail), c. 1830; St Peter's and St. Paul's Church, Shiplake, Oxfordshire, UK.

130 Giving a thirsty one something to drink (detail), Franz Mayer of Munich, Germany, 1910-1913; Cathedral Basilica of the Assumption, Covington, KY. Courtesy of the Cathedral Basilica of the Assumption, Covington, KY. Photograph © 2015 by St. Cecilia Congregation, LBP Communications. All rights reserved.

131 The Sacred Heart of Jesus (detail), Franz Mayer of Munich, Germany, 1910-1913; Cathedral Basilica of the Assumption, Coving-

ton, KY. Courtesy of the Cathedral Basilica of the Assumption, Covington, KY. Photograph © 2015 by St. Cecilia Congregation, LBP Communications. All rights reserved.

132 A Eucharistic procession (detail), Franz Mayer of Munich, Germany, 1910-1913; Cathedral Basilica of the Assumption, Covington, KY. Courtesy of the Cathedral Basilica of the Assumption, Covington, KY. Photograph © 2015 by St. Cecilia Congregation, LBP Communications. All rights reserved.

133 An angel adoring the Blessed Sacrament (detail), Franz Mayer of Munich, Germany, 1910-1913; Cathedral Basilica of the Assumption, Covington, KY. Courtesy of the Cathedral Basilica of the Assumption, Covington, KY. Photograph © 2015 by St. Cecilia Congregation, LBP Communications. All rights reserved.

134 The Nativity (detail), Franz Mayer of Munich, Germany, 1910-1913; Cathedral Basilica of the Assumption, Covington, KY. Courtesy of the Cathedral Basilica of the Assumption, Covington, KY. Photograph © 2015 by St. Cecilia Congregation, LBP Communications. All rights reserved.

135 Eucharistic Adoration (detail), Franz Mayer of Munich, Germany, 1910-1913; Cathedral Basilica of the Assumption, Covington, KY. Courtesy of the Cathedral Basilica of the Assumption, Covington, KY. Photograph © 2015 by St. Cecilia Congregation, LBP Communications. All rights reserved.

136-137 The miraculous Mass of St. Gregory (detail), Augustus Welby Pugin, c. 1884; St. Cuthbert's College, Ushaw, Ushaw Moor, Durham, UK.

138 St. Raphael leading Tobias (detail), Sir Ninian Comper, 1945; St. Alban the Martyr Church, Holborn, London, UK. Courtesy of the Parochial Church Council of St. Alban's, Holborn.

140-141 Hope, Charity, and Faith (detail), Edward Burne-Jones, c. 1891; St. Mary the Virgin, Buscot, Oxfordshire, UK.

142 St. Timothy (detail), Edward Burne-Jones, c. 1872; Christ Church Cathedral, Oxford, UK.

143 St. Timothy listening to his grandmother, Lois (detail), from the Vyner Memorial Window, Edward Burne-Jones, c. 1872; Christ Church Cathedral, Oxford, UK.

145 St. Dominic, Franz Mayer of Munich, Germany, 1910-1913; Cathedral Basilica of the Assumption, Covington, KY. Courtesy of the Cathedral Basilica of the Assumption, Covington, KY. Photograph © 2015 by St. Cecilia Congregation, LBP Communications. All rights reserved.

146 St. Ambrose, Franz Mayer of Munich, Germany, 1910-1913; Cathedral Basilica of the Assumption, Covington, KY. Courtesy of the Cathedral Basilica of the Assumption, Covington, KY. Photograph © 2015 by St. Cecilia Congregation, LBP Communications. All rights reserved.

147 St. Augustine, Franz Mayer of Munich, Germany, 1910-1913; Cathedral Basilica of the Assumption, Covington, KY. Courtesy of the Cathedral Basilica of the Assumption, Covington, KY. Photograph © 2015 by St. Cecilia Congregation, LBP Communications. All rights reserved.

148-149 Jesus raising the dead boy back to life (and detail), Franz Mayer of Munich, Germany, 1910-1913; Cathedral Basilica of the Assumption, Covington, KY. Courtesy of the Cathedral Basilica of the Assumption, Covington, KY. Photograph © 2015 by St. Cecilia Congregation, LBP Communications. All rights reserved.

150 St. Francis preaching to the birds (detail), c. 1920; Leicester Cathedral, St. Katherine's Chapel, Leicester, UK. Image used by permission of the Dean and Chapter of Leicester Cathedral.

151 The Christ Child (detail), Christopher Webb, c. 1940; St Alban's Cathedral, Hertfordshire, UK. Image used by permission of the Dean and Chapter of St. Alban's Cathedral.

152 The Rievaulx Abbey, Herbert Hendrie, c. 1928; Ampleforth Abbey, Ampleforth, UK. Courtesy of Ampleforth Abbey.

153 The Crucifixion (detail), Francis Spear, 1953; Glasgow Cathedral, Glasgow, UK. Courtesy of Glasgow Cathedral.

154-155 Jesus at the home of St. Martha and St. Mary (and detail), Charles Eamer Kempe, c.

1898; Christ Church, Newhaven, CT.

156 The Mother of Sorrows (detail), Charles Eamer Kempe, c. 1880s-90s; Priory Church of the Holy Trinity, Micklegate, York, UK.

157 The Crucified Christ (detail), Charles Eamer Kempe, c. 1880s-90s; Priory Church of the Holy Trinity, Micklegate, York, UK.

158 St. John the Evangelist, Charles Eamer Kempe, c. 1864; All Saints' Church, Cambridge, UK.

161 North rose window of the Virgin and Child surrounded by Old Testament themes (detail), c. 1250-60; Cathedral of Notre Dame, Paris, France.

171 St. Jerome (detail), c. 1884; Pembroke College Chapel, Oxford, UK.

172 Blessed Fra Angelico painting the Blessed Mother, c. 1883; St. Dominic's Priory Church, London, UK. Courtesy of St. Dominic's Priory Church, London, UK.

173 The Dominican coat of arms (detail), c. 1960; Rosary Priory, Bushey, Hertfordshire, UK. Courtesy of Rosary Priory, Bushey, Hertfordshire, UK.

173 Father Lawrence Lew, O.P., in the Edinburgh winter, January 19, 2013.

174 Three Dominican Sisters of St. Cecilia in Eucharistic Adoration, in the Chapel of St. Ce-

cilia, St. Cecilia Motherhouse, Nashville, Tennessee. Photograph © 2015 by St. Cecilia Congregation, LBP Communications. All rights reserved.

175 St. Cecilia (detail), (based on the painting by Raphael Sanzio, *The Ecstasy of St. Cecilia*, 1516–1517) F. X. Zettler of Munich, Germany, c. 1888; St. Cecilia Motherhouse Oratory, Nashville, Tennessee. Photograph © 2015 by St. Cecilia Congregation, LBP Communications. All rights reserved.

176 The Child Jesus and His Virgin Mother (detail), Franz Mayer of Munich, Germany, 1910-1913; Cathedral Basilica of the Assumption, Covington, KY. Courtesy of the Cathedral Basilica of the Assumption, Covington, KY. Photograph © 2015 by St. Cecilia Congregation, LBP Communications. All rights reserved.

BACK COVER: The multiplication of the loaves, Franz Mayer of Munich, Germany, 1910-1913; Cathedral Basilica of the Assumption, Covington, KY. Courtesy of the Cathedral Basilica of the Assumption, Covington, KY. Photograph © 2015 by St. Cecilia Congregation, LBP Communications. All rights reserved.

The author and publisher gratefully acknowledge the permission granted to reproduce the copyrighted material in this book.

Every effort has been made to trace copyright holders and to obtain their permission for the use of copyrighted material. The author and publisher apologize for any errors or omissions in the above list and would be grateful to be notified of any corrections that should be incorporated in future reprints or editions of this book.

ABOUT THE PHOTOGRAPHER:
FATHER LAWRENCE LEW, O.P.

A Dominican priest of the Province of England, Father Lawrence shares his love for beauty, and his talent for capturing it, through thousands of photographs of sacred art and architecture, of people, and of nature. Father Lawrence reflects, "I find that, as Hopkins said, 'the world is charged with the grandeur of God,' and so my photos might be likened to an offering of thanks to God for the goodness I see around me." His gift for photography is becoming more and more widely recognized. We are very grateful to Father Lawrence for his generosity in providing the stunning photographs of stained glass contained in this book.

ABOUT THE AUTHORS:
THE DOMINICAN SISTERS OF ST. CECILIA

Eight centuries ago, St. Dominic de Guzman, inspired by the Holy Spirit in response to the needs of his time, founded an Order with the mission of preaching for the salvation of souls. Dominic's love for God and neighbor continues to inspire the Dominican Sisters of St. Cecilia Congregation today, as they joyfully embrace the Church's call to the new evangelization. Founded in 1860 in Nashville, Tennessee, the Sisters live a contemplative-apostolic life of community, study, and apostolic service in a monastic framework that fosters contemplation. Through the apostolate of teaching, the Sisters have the privilege of serving students and families in the United States, Canada, Australia, Italy, Scotland, and the Netherlands. Under the protection and guidance of the Blessed Virgin Mary, the Sisters seek to live in fidelity to the Church and to bring others to Christ.

MARY,
QUEEN OF FAMILIES,
HELP OUR FAMILY
TO BE HOLY.
AMEN.